First World War
and Army of Occupation
War Diary
France, Belgium and Germany

21 DIVISION
62 Infantry Brigade
Northumberland Fusiliers
12/13th Battalion
1 August 1917 - 24 April 1919

WO95/2155/3

The Naval & Military Press Ltd
www.nmarchive.com
Published in association with The National Archives

Published by

The Naval & Military Press Ltd

Unit 10 Ridgewood Industrial Park,

Uckfield, East Sussex,

TN22 5QE England

Tel: +44 (0) 1825 749494

www.naval-military-press.com

www.nmarchive.com

This diary has been reprinted in facsimile from the original. Any imperfections are inevitably reproduced and the quality may fall short of modern type and cartographic standards.

© Crown Copyright
Images reproduced by permission of The National Archives, London, England, 2015.

Contents

Document type	Place/Title	Date From	Date To
Miscellaneous	WO95/2155-3		
Heading	21st Division 62nd Infy Bde. 12-13th Bn North'D Fus (Amalgamated Aug 1917 (Aug 1917-Apr 1919.		
War Diary	Boyelles	01/08/1917	07/08/1917
War Diary	Fontaine Lez-Croisilles.	09/08/1917	10/08/1917
War Diary	Moyenville	10/08/1917	10/08/1917
War Diary	Fontaine Lez Croisilles	17/08/1917	26/08/1917
War Diary	Croisilles	27/08/1917	31/08/1917
Miscellaneous			
Miscellaneous	Summary Of Patrol Reports For Week Ending August 25th 1917.	25/08/1917	25/08/1917
War Diary	Bn HQ M 35C 3.4	01/08/1917	01/08/1917
War Diary	Bn HQ Shaft Tr. T 6 C 10.20.	01/08/1917	04/08/1917
War Diary	Batt HQ. T6 b10.20.	05/08/1917	06/08/1917
War Diary	Bn. HQ Boyelles.	06/08/1917	07/08/1917
War Diary	Bn. H.Q. T22 d 6.9	08/08/1917	09/08/1917
War Diary	Moyenneville.	10/08/1917	10/08/1917
Map	Scale 1.20,000 Reference		
Map	3rd Field Survey Coy. R.E. (1395)		
Map	13th Bn. Northumberland Fusiliers Dispositions Aug 1st to Aug 6th 1917		
Map	Cigar Copse		
Miscellaneous	Nominal Roll Of Officers On Effective Strength		
Operation(al) Order(s)	12th (S) Bn Northumberland Fusiliers. Operation Order No 34.	05/08/1917	05/08/1917
Operation(al) Order(s)	13th Northumberland Fusiliers Operation Order No 46	05/08/1917	05/08/1917
Miscellaneous	O.C. 8th Leicester Regiment	09/08/1917	09/08/1917
Operation(al) Order(s)	13th Northumberland Fusrs Operation Order No 48	08/08/1917	08/08/1917
Operation(al) Order(s)	13th Northumberland Fusiliers Operation Order No 47	07/08/1917	07/08/1917
War Diary	Berneville	01/09/1917	17/09/1917
War Diary	Pradelles	18/09/1917	22/09/1917
War Diary	Le Roukloshille	23/09/1917	28/09/1917
War Diary	Westoutre.	29/09/1917	04/10/1917
War Diary	Polyeone Wood (de Zonnebeke)	04/10/1917	04/10/1917
War Diary	Near Reutel	04/10/1917	07/10/1917
War Diary	La Belle Hotesse.	08/10/1917	10/10/1917
War Diary	Ypres	11/10/1917	25/10/1917
War Diary	Zillebeke	25/10/1917	26/10/1917
War Diary	Noordemdhoek	27/10/1917	31/10/1917
Operation(al) Order(s)	12/13th Bn Northumberland Fusiliers Operation Order No. 9	02/10/1917	02/10/1917
Operation(al) Order(s)	12/13th Northumberland Fusiliers Operation Order No 13	18/10/1917	18/10/1917
Miscellaneous	C.O. 12/13th North. Fusrs. Goldfish Chateau.	17/10/1917	17/10/1917
Operation(al) Order(s)	Relief Orders No 2 by Major H.C.O Cannon. M.C.	25/10/1917	25/10/1917
Operation(al) Order(s)	12/13th Northumberland Fusiliers Operation Order No 15	25/10/1917	25/10/1917
Operation(al) Order(s)	12/13th Northumberland Fusiliers Administration Order No 1.	25/10/1917	25/10/1917
War Diary	Zillebeke.	01/11/1917	04/11/1917

War Diary	Clapham Junction.	05/11/1917	07/11/1917
War Diary	Reutel.	08/11/1917	12/11/1917
War Diary	Zillebeke	13/11/1917	13/11/1917
War Diary	Hallebast.	14/11/1917	15/11/1917
War Diary	Westoutre	16/11/1917	17/11/1917
War Diary	Vieux Berquin.	18/11/1917	18/11/1917
War Diary	Annezin.	19/11/1917	19/11/1917
War Diary	Hersin	20/11/1917	20/11/1917
War Diary	Mont St Eloi	21/11/1917	21/11/1917
War Diary	Maroeuil.	22/11/1917	30/11/1917
War Diary	Peronne	01/12/1917	01/12/1917
War Diary	Longavesnes	03/12/1917	08/12/1917
War Diary	Peziere	09/12/1917	17/12/1917
War Diary	Heudicourt.	18/12/1917	31/12/1917
Miscellaneous	12/13th Northumberland Fusiliers. Defence Scheme Etc. Appendix No 1	13/12/1917	13/12/1917
Map	Appendix No 2 From Sheet 57C. S.E 4		
Operation(al) Order(s)	12/13th Northumberland Fusiliers Operation Order No. 35 Appx No 3	12/12/1917	12/12/1917
Miscellaneous	Administrative Orders.		
Miscellaneous	Right Sub Sector Left Brigade. Defence Scheme. "Bear" Appendix No 3		
Operation(al) Order(s)	Operation Order No. 36 Appx 4	16/12/1917	16/12/1917
Miscellaneous		16/12/1917	16/12/1917
Heading	Bear Defences Scheme		
Miscellaneous	Right Sub-Sector Bear Left Brigade Appx 6	16/12/1917	16/12/1917
Miscellaneous	Appendix No 6		
Map	Appendix No 5 From Sheet 57c. SE 4 Scale 1/10000		
Miscellaneous	Administrative Orders. Appx 4	16/12/1917	16/12/1917
Miscellaneous	Appendix No 7		
Miscellaneous	Defence Scheme 12/13th Northumberland Fusiliers Appx 8	17/12/1917	17/12/1917
Miscellaneous	Appendix No 8		
Operation(al) Order(s)	12/13th Northumberland Fusiliers. Operation Order No. 38 Appx 9	24/12/1917	24/12/1917
Miscellaneous	Administrative Instructions.	26/12/1917	26/12/1917
Miscellaneous	Instructions.	25/12/1917	25/12/1917
War Diary	Heudicourt.	01/01/1918	31/01/1918
Operation(al) Order(s)	Operation Order No. 41 Appx. 1	01/01/1918	01/01/1918
Operation(al) Order(s)	12/13th Northumberland Fusiliers Administrative Orders To Accompany Operation Order No 52. Appendix 2	17/02/1918	17/02/1918
Miscellaneous	Bear Administrative Orders. Appx 2	01/01/1918	01/01/1918
Miscellaneous	Orders.		
Miscellaneous	Defence Arrangements Support Battalion Appx 3	03/01/1918	03/01/1918
Operation(al) Order(s)	Bear Operation Order No. 42 Appx 4	07/01/1918	07/01/1918
Miscellaneous	Administrative Instructions Appx 4	07/01/1918	07/01/1918
Operation(al) Order(s)	Operation Order No. 43 Appx 5	10/01/1918	10/01/1918
Miscellaneous	Bear Defence Scheme. Appx 6	09/01/1918	09/01/1918
Operation(al) Order(s)	Operation Order No. 44 Appx 4	11/01/1918	11/01/1918
Operation(al) Order(s)	Operation Order No. 45 Appx 8	15/01/1918	15/01/1918
Miscellaneous	Administrative Orders.	15/01/1918	15/01/1918
Miscellaneous	Administrative Orders.	19/01/1918	19/01/1918
Miscellaneous	Programme Of Work.	15/01/1918	15/01/1918
Operation(al) Order(s)	Operation Order No. 47 Appx 9	19/01/1918	19/01/1918
Operation(al) Order(s)	Operation Order No. 48 Appx 10	23/01/1918	23/01/1918
Miscellaneous	Administrative Orders.	23/01/1918	23/01/1918

Type	Description	Start	End
Operation(al) Order(s)	Operation Order No 49 Appx 11	25/01/1918	25/01/1918
Miscellaneous	Amendment To Operation Order No. 49	26/01/1918	26/01/1918
Operation(al) Order(s)	Operation Order No 50 Appendix No 12	27/01/1918	27/01/1918
Miscellaneous	Administrative Orders	27/01/1918	27/01/1918
Miscellaneous	Preliminary Orders for move tomorrow	29/01/1918	29/01/1918
Operation(al) Order(s)	12/13th Northumberland Fusiliers Operation Order No 51. Appendix 1	06/02/1918	06/02/1918
War Diary	Moislains	01/02/1918	06/02/1918
War Diary	Templeux-La-Fosse.	07/02/1918	18/02/1918
War Diary	Moislains.	19/02/1918	28/02/1918
Miscellaneous	O.C. A.B.C.D & H.Q. T.O. & Q.M.	27/02/1918	27/02/1918
Operation(al) Order(s)	12/13th Northumberland Fusiliers Operation Order No 52 Appendix 2	17/02/1918	17/02/1918
Operation(al) Order(s)	12/13th Northumberland Fusiliers Administrative Instructions to accompany Operation Order No 54	27/02/1918	27/02/1918
Operation(al) Order(s)	12/13th Northumberland Fusiliers Operation Order No 54 Appx 3	27/02/1918	27/02/1918
Map	Appendix No. 10 From Sheet 57C SE 4		
Heading	62nd Inf. Bde. 21st Div. War Diary 12th/13th Battn. The Northumberland Fusiliers. March 1918		
War Diary	Trenches. Heudecourt.	01/03/1918	21/03/1918
War Diary	Green Line to Bray	22/03/1918	25/03/1918
War Diary	Bray	26/03/1918	26/03/1918
War Diary	Bray Ribemont	27/03/1918	31/03/1918
Heading	62nd Brigade. 21st Division. 12/13th Battalion Northumberland Fusiliers April 1918.		
War Diary	Hangest	01/04/1918	01/04/1918
War Diary	Locre	02/04/1918	03/04/1918
War Diary	Wytschaete Reserve	04/04/1918	07/04/1918
War Diary	Locre	08/04/1918	10/04/1918
War Diary	Line Wytschaete	11/04/1918	12/04/1918
War Diary	Regent St Dugouts Irish Honse	13/04/1918	15/04/1918
War Diary	Line Wytschaete	16/04/1918	16/04/1918
War Diary	Wytschaete	17/04/1918	18/04/1918
War Diary	Siege Farm	19/04/1918	19/04/1918
War Diary	Ouderdom	20/04/1918	25/04/1918
War Diary	Line Ridge Wood	26/04/1918	26/04/1918
War Diary	Ouderdom.	27/04/1918	28/04/1918
War Diary	Steenvoorde	29/04/1918	30/04/1918
War Diary	Lederzeele Area	01/05/1918	04/05/1918
War Diary	Lhery	05/05/1918	11/05/1918
War Diary	Lhery to Vaux-Yarennes Line	13/05/1918	15/05/1918
War Diary	Berry-Au-Bac	16/05/1918	27/05/1918
War Diary	Pevy	28/05/1918	30/05/1918
War Diary	Vaucinnes	31/05/1918	31/05/1918
Operation(al) Order(s)	Bear Operation Order No 11	24/05/1918	24/05/1918
Operation(al) Order(s)	12/13 Northumberland Fusiliers Operation Order No 5	03/05/1918	03/05/1918
Operation(al) Order(s)	12/13th Northumberland Fusiliers Operation Order No 7	11/05/1918	11/05/1918
Operation(al) Order(s)	12/13th Northumberland Fusiliers Operation Order No 8	13/05/1918	13/05/1918
Operation(al) Order(s)	Bear. Operation Order No 9	17/05/1918	17/05/1918
Operation(al) Order(s)	Bear Operation Order No 10	20/05/1918	20/05/1918
War Diary	Soulieres	01/06/1918	02/06/1918
War Diary	Villevenard	03/06/1918	08/06/1918
War Diary	La Nocre	09/06/1918	14/06/1918
War Diary	Longpres	15/06/1918	15/06/1918
War Diary	Hallencourt	16/06/1918	17/06/1918

War Diary	Senarpont.	18/06/1918	20/06/1918
War Diary	Grandcourt	21/06/1918	01/07/1918
War Diary	Beauquesne	07/07/1918	12/07/1918
Miscellaneous	A Form Messages And Signals.		
War Diary	Beauquesne	12/07/1918	13/07/1918
War Diary	Toutencourt	14/07/1918	17/07/1918
War Diary	Arqueves	18/07/1918	23/07/1918
War Diary	In The Line	24/07/1918	28/07/1918
War Diary	In Reserve	29/07/1918	29/07/1918
War Diary	Acheux	30/07/1918	31/07/1918
War Diary	Purple Line.	01/08/1918	03/08/1918
War Diary	Beaussart	04/08/1918	08/08/1918
War Diary	Purple Line.	09/08/1918	10/08/1918
War Diary	In The Line	11/08/1918	16/08/1918
War Diary	Purple System	17/08/1918	20/08/1918
War Diary	In The Line	21/08/1918	28/08/1918
War Diary	Bde. Reserve	29/08/1918	31/08/1918
War Diary	Brigade Reserve.	01/09/1918	14/09/1918
War Diary	Reserve.	15/09/1918	15/09/1918
War Diary	In The Line.	16/09/1918	19/09/1918
War Diary	Reserve	20/09/1918	25/09/1918
War Diary	In The Line	26/09/1918	28/09/1918
War Diary	Bde Reserve	29/09/1918	30/09/1918
Heading	War Diary 12/13th Bn Northumberland Fusiliers. October 1st-31st 1918. Vol 38		
War Diary	Brigade Reserve	01/10/1918	01/10/1918
War Diary	NE Gonnelieu	02/10/1918	03/10/1918
War Diary	Gauzeacourt.	04/10/1918	04/10/1918
War Diary	In The Line	05/10/1918	08/10/1918
War Diary	Walincourt.	09/10/1918	21/10/1918
War Diary	In The Line.	22/10/1918	26/10/1918
War Diary	Neuvilly.	27/10/1918	28/10/1918
War Diary	In The Line	29/10/1918	31/10/1918
War Diary	Brigade Reserve	01/10/1918	01/10/1918
War Diary	NE Gonnelieu	02/10/1918	03/10/1918
War Diary	Gauzeacourt	04/10/1918	05/10/1918
War Diary	In The Line	06/10/1918	08/10/1918
War Diary	Walincourt.	09/10/1918	21/10/1918
War Diary	In The Line	22/10/1918	26/10/1918
War Diary	Neuvilly.	27/10/1918	28/10/1918
War Diary	In The Line	29/10/1918	31/10/1918
Heading	War Diary Of 12/13th Bn Northumberland Fusiliers. From 1st November 1918 To 30th November 1918 Vol 39		
War Diary	In Reserve	01/11/1918	04/11/1918
War Diary	In The Line.	05/11/1918	06/11/1918
War Diary	Aymeries "Belgium & Part Of France" Sheet 51. U.16	07/11/1918	11/11/1918
War Diary	Bachant "Belgium & Part Of France" Sheet 51 U.18.	12/11/1918	15/11/1918
War Diary	Aymeries	16/11/1918	30/11/1918
Heading	War Diary Of 12/13th Bn Northumberland Fusiliers. From 1st December 1918 To 31st December 1918 Vol 40		
War Diary	Aymeries	01/12/1918	17/12/1918
War Diary	Englefontaine	18/12/1918	18/12/1918
War Diary	Inchy	19/12/1918	19/12/1918
War Diary	Fourdrinoy	20/12/1918	31/12/1918

Heading	War Diary Of 12/13th Bn. Northumberland Fusiliers. From 1st January 1919. To 31st January 1919. Vol 41		
War Diary	Foudrinoy.	01/01/1919	31/01/1919
Heading	War Diary Of 12/13th Bn Northumberland Fusiliers. From 1st February 1919. To 28th February 1919 Vol 42		
War Diary	Fourdrinoy	01/02/1919	06/02/1919
War Diary	Fourdrin	07/02/1919	13/02/1919
War Diary	Fourdrinoy.	13/02/1919	05/04/1919
War Diary	Bouchon	05/04/1919	24/04/1919
War Diary	Bouchon. And Longpre.	24/04/1919	24/04/1919

No 95/2155/3

21ST DIVISION
62ND INFY BDE.

12-13TH BN NORTH'D FUS
(AMALGAMATED AUG 1917

(AUG 1917 - APR 1919.

WAR DIARY
or
INTELLIGENCE SUMMARY

Army Form C. 2118.

12/13th Bn Northumberland Fusiliers

Vol 24

Place	Date	Hour	Summary of Events and Information	Remarks and references to Appendices
BOYELLES	July 1st 1917		The 12th Battalion Northumberland Fusiliers relieved the 10th Battn. YORKSHIRE REGT in the Right subsector of the left Bde front; "B" Coy C Coy on the right holding from a point U.7.B.10.75. on the SENSEE River, D Coy in the centre and B company on the left, holding to a point U.1.A.4.6. at the junction of CLAW trench and the PUG AVENUE. A Company in support in the old Hindenburg support front line (KIND trench). The relief was completed by 11.30 A.M. without casualties. The Battalion on the right was the 15th Battn. Durham Light Infantry, on the left the 13th Battn. Northumberland Fusiliers, 62nd Bde.	51. B.S.W. 1/20,000
	2 - 5		The enemy were unusually quiet, no casualties were suffered, our patrols constantly forward the enemy and dispersed his wiring parties; the hostile artillery was very inactive, and except for a few aerial duels the enemy showed no activity against us.	
	6.		The 63rd Bde took over the subsector South of the SENSEE River, the 1st Battn. LINCOLNSHIRE Regt coming in on the right of the 12th Northld Fusiliers in place of the 15th Battn. Durham Light Infantry; on the left the 149th Bde took over the subsector held by the 13th Battn Northld Fusiliers and the 9th Battn Durham Light Infantry came up on the left of the 12th Battn. Northld Fusiliers.	
	7.		A quiet day, the enemy shelled CLAW trench with 77mm and 115mm shells, but did	

WAR DIARY
or
INTELLIGENCE SUMMARY

(Erase heading not required.)

Army Form C. 2118.

Place	Date	Hour	Summary of Events and Information	Remarks and references to Appendices
Fonteure LE2 CROISILLES	Aug 9		No damage and caused no casualties. The 12th Battalion Northumberland Fusiliers relieved by the 7th Batt LEICESTERSHIRE REGT 110 Bde, the relief was completed by 4.30 pm without casualties. The 12th Battalion moved to 7 Camp at MOYENVILLE.	
	Aug 10		The 12th & 13th Battalions Northumberland Fusiliers were amalgamated, to be called hereafter the 12/13 Batt. Northumberland Fusiliers. The following officers were appointed officers of the new Battalion, to be called hereafter Northumberland Fusiliers.	

The following is a list of H.Q. and Specialist Officers, Company Officers

Lieut. Col. S.H. Dixon M.C. (13.) Commanding Officer
Major F.G.E. Follmann D.S.O. (12.) 2nd in Command
Capt. J. White M.C. (12.) Adjutant
Capt. J.A. Dubedat (13.) Assistant Adjutant
Lieut. J. McKinnon (12.) Lewis Gun Officer
Lieut. H. Bergin (13.) Transport
Lieut. J.H. Pleet D.S.O. M.C. (12.) Patrol Officer
2nd Lieut. J.H. Fessenden (13.) Intelligence Officer
1st Lieut. R.A. Brennan (12.) Bombing Officer
2nd Lieut. J.L. South (13.) Sniping Officer
2nd Lieut. J.H. Brunswick (12.) Signals
Lieut. H.W. Ingham (13.) Lewis Officer
Lieut. & R.H. J. Seldon (13.) Quartermaster

Capt. E.H. Griffin M.C. (attached) Medical Officer
Rev. B.F. Marshall M.C. Chaplain

Army Form C. 2118.

WAR DIARY
or
INTELLIGENCE SUMMARY
(Erase heading not required.)

Place	Date	Hour	Summary of Events and Information	Remarks and references to Appendices
Bus	10th (contd)		"A" Coy. Capt. J. Lockie M.C. 12th Batln. Capt. J.H. Herbert. 13. " 2nd Lieut G.H. Edmonds. 12. " 2nd Lieut P.J. Gregory. 12. " 2nd Lieut W.H. Lithbridge 13. " 2nd Lieut E.J. Garland. 13. " "B" Coy. Capt. G.R. Riddell 13. " Lieut J.O. Byrne 12. " 2nd Lieut C.A. Wilson 13. " 2nd Lieut H.J. Jackson. 13. " 2nd Lieut J.W. Elliott 12. " 2nd Lieut W.C. Dickinson. 12. " "C" Coy. Capt. J. Bownton M.C. 12th Batln. Capt. A. Rutherford. 13. " 2nd Lieut A.J. Clifford. 13. " 2nd Lieut V.C. Chapman. 13. " 2nd Lieut W.E. Waistell 12. " 2nd Lieut J. Thomas. 12. " "D" Coy. Capt. H. Graham 13 Batln. Lieut J. Sedgwick. 12. " 2nd Lieut R. Lummis 13. " 2nd Lieut H. Partington 13. " 2nd Lieut F.A. Irwin. 12. " 2nd Lieut R.C. Alford. 12. " This concludes the diary of the 12th Batln. Northumberland Fusiliers on a separate unit. J.McIlwain Major. Commanding 12th Batln. Northumberland Fusiliers	

Army Form C. 2118.

WAR DIARY
or
INTELLIGENCE SUMMARY
(Erase heading not required.)

Place	Date	Hour	Summary of Events and Information	Remarks and references to Appendices
MOYENVILLE	Aug 10 1917		The 12/13th Battalion Northumberland Fusiliers was organized as a Battalion from the 12th and 13th Battalions Northumberland Fusiliers. The new Battalion remained at 't' camp at MOYENVILLE during the process of reorganization which was practically completed by Aug 17. The effective strength of the new Battalion was limited to 750 O.R. exclusive of N.C.O's of the rank of full Corporal & upwards. In consequence 312 O.R were despatched to ETAPLES as reinforcements for other units of the Regiment. Parties of 150 O.R were conducted to ETAPLES by Major EDLMANN D.S.O on Aug 17. On this date the 12/13 Battn moved up to the left sector of the 13th Bde front and took over from the 7th Battn LEICESTERSHIRE REGT from the SENSEE River at a point U.7.B.10.75 to a point U.1.A.4.6 at the junction of CLAW and PUG AVENUE. The 10th Battn the Yorkshire REGT was on the right and the 30th Division on the left. Battalion Headquarters were situated in the HINDENBURG TUNNEL at T.6.d.40.98. A & B Coy held the front line, D Coy the centre and C Coy the left company sector in the front line.	Ref Map 51.B.S.W. 1/20,000
FONTAINE LEZ CROISILLES	Aug 17.		B was in support in the old HINDENBURG front line (HIND Trench). The evening & night were quiet. Our patrols examined No mans Land during the night, and saw of the enemy was found on our side of his wire. Weather fine and dry.	

Army Form C. 2118.

WAR DIARY
or
INTELLIGENCE SUMMARY

(Erase heading not required.)

Instructions regarding War Diaries and Intelligence Summaries are contained in F. S. Regs., Part II. and the Staff Manual respectively. Title Pages will be prepared in manuscript.

Place	Date	Hour	Summary of Events and Information	Remarks and references to Appendices
FONTAINE LEZ CROISILLES	Aug 18.		Hostile artillery rather active, but caused no damage or casualties.	Ref Map 51. B.S.W 1/20.000
	19.		Our patrols were again very active by night. The 2 sent out joined "Fuzes" in the VII Corps Minefuze. Slow in the 2nd four animal and 2nd fuze with short instead was far. The enemy were again active with artillery fire but our fire failed to do any damage. Lt S. Philip, D.S.O.M.G. The enemy were again within 60 yards of the enemy's trenches by daylight & returned safely with valuable information. Capt D. E. WRIGHT conducted a further party of 1 S.D.O.R to ETAPLES.	
	20.		A very quiet day. Our artillery carried out a shoot against FONTAINE and FONTAINE WOOD. 1st Sedgewick transferred to 15th Batln Durham Light Infantry. There was no hostile retaliation.	
	21.		Another very quiet day. 2nd Lt T. W. WILKINSON reported from the 3rd Batln North'd Fusiliers was taken on strength.	
	22.		The Battalion was relieved by the 3/4 QUEENS ROYAL WEST SURREY REGT, a new Battalion from England to replace the 13 H Batln Northumberland Fusiliers in the 62nd Bde. The relief was completed at 4.15 p.m.; no casualties were suffered during the tour of duty in trenches. The Battalion went into Bde Reserve behind CROISILLES with Battn Headquarters at T.23.d.6.19.	
	23.		Uneventful day. The Battalion found large working parties for the trenches. 2nd Lt A. E. WOODS arrived and was posted to D Coy. Hon Lieut & Quartermaster J. WELDON left for the Base.	
	24.25 26.		Battalion in Bde reserve; no hostile shelling; weather wet and windy.	

Army Form C. 2118.

WAR DIARY
or
INTELLIGENCE SUMMARY
(Erase heading not required.)

Instructions regarding War Diaries and Intelligence Summaries are contained in F. S. Regs., Part II. and the Staff Manual respectively. Title Pages will be prepared in manuscript.

Place	Date	Hour	Summary of Events and Information	Remarks and references to Appendices
CROISILLES	Aug 27.		The Battalion returned in Bde Reserve by the 9th Battalion ROYAL DUBLIN FUSILIERS, 16th Irish Division. Relief complete by 4 p.m in torrential rain; the Battalion moved to camp near HAMELINCOURT on the HAMELINCOURT – BOISLEUX – AU – MONT road. During the night there was a severe gale and considerable damage was done to the camp. At 10 A.M the Battalion marched to BERNEVILLE, arriving there at 1 A.M. and went into good REST billets there.	Ref/Map ST.O.S.W. 20.OTO
	28			
	29-31		Reorganisation and Battalion training carried out. Capt J. LOCKIE M.C and Capt J. BRUNTON M.C were granted a month's leave of absence. Capt D.F.J. Wasper took command of A Coy and Capt Rutherford of C. Coy. The Coys were reorganised on the basis of 3 platoons per Company.	

J.M.S. Murra Major
for Lt Col Commanding
1/10 Batln Northumberland Fusiliers

- 2 -

    (ii)   At U.1.b.45.30 the wire is thin.

    (iii)   Between U.13.b.9.9 and U.14.a.7.1 there is a strong belt and no gaps were seen.

    (iv)   A thick belt of wire runs round the S. and W. side of enemy post at U.1.d.9.1 and a thin belt runs N. towards SENSEE TRENCH.

    (v)   Wire at U.1.b.3.4 consists of a single belt of apron wire. None was seen between U.20.b.5.7 and U.21.a.4.6.

    (vi)   There is a gap at U.7.b.5.2.

(b) <u>Our Own.</u>

    (i)   In front of SHAFT TRENCH, immediately N. of SENSEE RIVER, the outer belt of our wire consists of concertina which will form a good obstacle when the somewhat numerous gaps are made good.

    (ii)   The wire at U.1.c.4.6 is reported thin.

SECRET.

21 Div.
G.1650.

SUMMARY OF PATROL REPORTS
FOR WEEK ENDING AUGUST 25TH 1917.

1.   The undermentioned Officers and O.R. rendered valuable reports during the period under review:

62nd Infantry Brigade.

```
Lieut. G.M.Phillip, B.S.O., M.C. )
2/Lt.  R.Chapman,                )
  :    A.G.Clifford,             )
  :    G.M.Edmonds,              )
  :    W.H.Lethbridge,           )  12/13th North'd Fus.
  :    R.Lummis,                 )
  :    G.Thomas,                 )
  :    F.H.Urwin,                )
  :    W.E.Waistell,             )
```

WAR DIARY
or
INTELLIGENCE SUMMARY.
(Erase heading not required.)

Army Form C. 2118.

Place	Date	Hour	Summary of Events and Information	Remarks and references to Appendices

Bn HQ M35 c 3.4	Aug. 1		In the trenches — Quiet day, no shelling. The 13th Bn. relieved the 12th Bn Lincolnshire Regt. in the front line, left subsector, this evening. Dispositions of the battalion were as follows:—
			
			 Bn. H.Q. SNIPE TR. T 6 c 10.20
			 Right Company (A Company) U1 a 10.65
			 Centre Company (B Company) O 31 c 30.50
			 Left Company (C Company) O 31 c 80.60
			 Support Company (D Company) M 36 d 20.20.
			
			 Posts:
			 I Right Company.
			  No. 10 Post PUG AVENUE U 1 a 65.55
			  No. 11 — PUG AVENUE U 1 a 50.55
			  No. 12 — BUSH TRENCH U 1 a 25.90
			  No. 13 — RUSH TRENCH U 1 a 40.90
			
			 II Centre Company.
			  No. 14 Post DODO TRENCH U 1 a 85.90
			  No. 15 — DODO TRENCH O 31 c 85.05
			  No. 16 — ROTTEN ROW U 1 b 30.90
			
			 III Left Company.
			  No. 17 Post WOOD TR. O 31 d 40.00
			
			 III Left Company (Cont.)
			  No. 18 Post SNIPE TR. U 1 c 55.95
			  No. 19 Post SNIPE TR. O 31 d 60.10
			  Support hqrs. SNIPE TR. O 31 d 50.40
			
			 IV Support Company
			  1 Platoon in dug-out at M 36 d 80.40
			  1 Platoon in dug-out at T 6 a 80.90.
			  Support Platoon (Centre Company)
			  SHALLOON LANE O 31 c 50.70.
				Very wet day.

WAR DIARY
or
INTELLIGENCE SUMMARY.
(Erase heading not required.)

Army Form C. 2118.

Place	Date	Hour	Summary of Events and Information	Remarks and references to Appendices
Bn. HQ SHAFT TR. T.6.C.10.20.	Aug 1 (cont)		The relief took place without special incident. There were some slight shelling about 6 pm and half-a-dozen rounds were fired into SHAFT TR. About 9.20 pm. 7 heavy trench mortars fell in DODO TR — 3 casualties. Companies wiring.	
Bn. HQ SHAFT TR. T.6.C.10.20.	Aug 2		In the trenches — Between 2 am & 2.20 am. 20 apparently blind shells fell E. of PELICAN LANE. The force of goo observed. Our snipers busy in afternoon. There was a heavy bombardment by our artillery on the other enemy works in front of SNIPE TR. at 3 p.m. The enemy retaliated and about 100 rounds of 10 cm & HE shrapnel were fired into the vicinity of BUSH, CLAW, TR's & PUG AVENUE. Patrol from left company under 2nd Lt Clifford patrolled toward gun pits. A patrol from centre company under 2nd Lt. Les patrolled ROTTEN ROW and reached within 10 yds of the Gun pits. Patrols was fired on. 2nd Lieut Los Corporal Whitaker missing, believed wounded. A patrol under 2nd Lieut R Lumais went out from ROTTEN old pit in PUG AVENUE with object of recovering the missing officer and corporal. Patrol fired on from gun pits and Corporal Kelling wounded. Companies wiring and improving trenches.	Quell and showery

WAR DIARY or INTELLIGENCE SUMMARY

Army Form C. 2118.

Place	Date	Hour	Summary of Events and Information	Remarks and references to Appendices
Bn. H.Q. SHAFT TR. T.6.b.10.20.	Aug. 3rd.		In the Trenches:— Enemy extraordinarily quiet today. The tank was destroyed by us at 2 a.m. Trench mortars were fairly active. Enemy bombarded the junction of DODO & BUSH TRENCHES with aerial darts and light Trench Mortars between 6.20 and 6.40 p.m. Some short rounds from our 18 pounders fell in WOOD TR., SNIPE TR., & now our forward posts in PUG AVENUE. Our snipers claim 1 hit. A patrol under 2nd Lt. Clifford went out from left company. A patrol under 2nd Lt. Kinnin went out from ROTTEN ROW Post in search of missing officer and corporal. No result. 2nd Lieut Col. Stephenson and 2nd Lieut G.M. Newton joined the Battalion today.	Dull and wet
Bn. H.Q. SHAFT TR. T.6 & 10.20.	Aug. 4th		In the Trenches:— Enemy artillery fairly quiet. Over twenty 7.7 cm shells fell in the neighbourhood of TANK TR. and BROWN SUPPORT between 2.11 and June 2.30 p.m. Between 8.45 p.m and 9 p.m. several aerial darts and a few heavy T.M.S. fell near our forward posts in PUG AVENUE and ROTTEN ROW. About 11.30 p.m. Showery a wiring party from 10th Yorks. Regt. were fired on by the enemy and three casualties were caused. 2nd Lieut Clifford with three of our men assisted in bringing in the wounded. A patrol from the left company went out	Cold.

Army Form C. 2118.

WAR DIARY
or
INTELLIGENCE SUMMARY.
(Erase heading not required.)

Instructions regarding War Diaries and Intelligence Summaries are contained in F. S. Regs., Part II. and the Staff Manual respectively. Title pages will be prepared in manuscript.

Place	Date	Hour	Summary of Events and Information	Remarks and references to Appendices
			From SNIPE TR. Companies wiring and improving trenches. 2/Lieuts M. Darling, H.J. Jebron, H.J. James, and O.L. Mould joined the battalion today.	
Batt. I.H.Q. T.6.b.10.20	Aug 5th		In the Trenches :- Hostile artillery fairly quiet. Between 10 am and 10.20 am about 30 rounds 7.7 cm fell near the junction of SNIPE TR. and BROWN SUPPORT. At 4.15 am 6 heavy T.M's fell near DODO TR. and retaliation was asked for. About 8 am the enemy fired about 30 or 40 aerial darts in the vicinity of No 10 post in PUG AVENUE, and DODO TR. Our snipers fairly active. A patrol under Sergt NUNTER went out from the left company at 11 p.m. Reported an abandoned post. MOOD TR still unoccupied. Enemy connecting his forward trench and the outposts. Companies wiring and improving trenches.	Fine and bright.
Batt.H.Q. T.6.b.10.20	Aug 6th		In the trenches :- Hostile artillery very quiet. Today the regiment of the Divisional front was commenced. The 151st Inf. Brig. relieved the	Dull & showery.

T2134. Wt. W708-776. 500000. 4/15. Sir J. C. & S.

WAR DIARY
or
INTELLIGENCE SUMMARY.

(Erase heading not required.)

Army Form C. 2118.

Place	Date	Hour	Summary of Events and Information	Remarks and references to Appendices
	Aug 6th (cont)		62nd Inf Brig. North of the PUG AVENUE - SHAFT TR & its junction with TSKANH SUPPORT. 9th Bn. Durham Light Infantry relieved the 13th Bn. Northumberland Fusiliers in the Line Left Subsector (two posts in PUG AVENUE). 12th Bn. Northumberland Fusiliers	
Bn. H.Q.			relieved 13th Bn. North'd Fus in the posts in PUG AVENUE. Dispositions of the	and dry.
BOYELLES.			Battalion after relief were as follows. "B" Coy in HIND TR. between FULDMER & FIT LANE. "B" Coy in the Posts C6 & C10 (both inclusive) "C" Coy, "D" Coy & H.Q. in the camp at BOYELLES.	
Bn. H.Q. BOYELLES	Aug 7th		In the Trenches. 13th Bn. North'd Fus. relieved the 10th Bn. King's Own Yorkshire Light Infantry (less two companies) in Brigade support in the evening. "A" Coy relieved 1 Coy K.O.Y.L.I. in the Quarry T.1.8.6 at 7 p.m. "C" Coy relieved 1 Coy K.O.Y.L.I. in the Sunken Road T.23 a. H.Q. moved from BOYELLES to T.22.d.6.9. Relief was complete by 8 p.m.	Bright teenager weather.
Bn. H.Q. T.22.d.6.9	Aug 8th		In the Trenches. Dispositions of Companies. "D" Coy in HIND TR between FULDMER LANE & FIT LANE. "B" Coy in posts C6 & C10 (inclusive)	

WAR DIARY
or
INTELLIGENCE SUMMARY.
(Erase heading not required.)

Army Form C. 2118.

Place	Date	Hour	Summary of Events and Information	Remarks and references to Appendices
	Aug. 8 (cont)		"A" Coy in the Quarry at T.18.b. "C" Coy in the Sunken Road at T.23.a. The Commanding Officer visited the 12th Bn. Headquarters this morning. A very heavy thunderstorm in the evening flooded many of the dug-outs and shelters.	Fine in morning. Thunderstorm in the evening.
Bn. H.Q. T.22.d 6.9	Aug. 9		In the Trenches:- Quiet day, no shelling. The 13th Bn. Northumberland Fusiliers were relieved by the 8th Bn. Leicestershire Regt. at about 3.30 p.m. The battalion on being relieved marched to Camp "B" Moyenneville.	Fine and Bright.
MOYENNEVILLE.	Aug. 10th		In Rest. The 12th and 13th Battalions Northumberland Fusiliers were amalgamated today, the new battalion to be known as 12/13 Bn. Northumberland Fusiliers. The 13th Bn. N.F. on being moved across by companies in the morning to "Y" Camp. The following companies were amalgamated:- "A" Coy } of the 13th Bn. and "A" Coy } of the 13th Bn. "C" Coy " " " " "B" Coy " " " " "B" Coy " " " " "C" Coy " " " " "D" Coy " " " " "D" Coy " " " "	Bright Sunny day.

Place	Date	Hour	Summary of Events and Information	Remarks and references to Appendices
	Aug. 10 (cont)		The following is a list of H.Q. and specialist Officers, Company Officers.	

Lieut. Col. S.A. Box MC (13th) Commanding Officer.
Major J.J. Ellwain D.S.O. (12th) 2nd in Command
Captain G. White M.C. (12th) Adjutant
Captain J.A. Ockshott (13th) Assistant Adjutant
Lieut J. McKinnon (12th) Lewis Gun Officer.
Lieut W. Bowie (13th) Transport
Lieut G.M. Philip D.S.O. M.C. (12th) Patrol Officer.
2nd Lieut J.H. Heggelu (13th) Intelligence Officer
2nd Lieut R.A. Briance (12th) Bombing Officer.
2nd Lieut J.H. Lowth (13th) Sniping Officer.
2nd Lieut E.H. Bramwell (12th) Signals
Lieut O.H.O. Jackson (13th) Works Officer.
Lieut & Qr.Mr. J. Weldon (13th) Quartermaster

Captain E.A. Griffin M.C. (attached) Medical Officer
Rev. B.J. Marshall M.C. Chaplain.

Army Form C. 2118.

WAR DIARY
or
INTELLIGENCE SUMMARY.
(Erase heading not required.)

Instructions regarding War Diaries and Intelligence Summaries are contained in F. S. Regs., Part II. and the Staff Manual respectively. Title pages will be prepared in manuscript.

Place	Date	Hour	Summary of Events and Information	Remarks and references to Appendices
	Aug 6 (cont)		"A" Coy. Captain J. Yorkie M.C. Captain Th. Herbert. 2nd Lieut G.R. Edmonds 2nd Lieut P.G. Gregory. 2nd Lieut A.S.M. Lethbridge 2nd Lieut E.J. Garland. "B" Coy. Captain G.B. Riddell Lieut J.O. Byrne. 2nd Lieut C.R. Wilson 2nd Lieut H.J. Jackson 2nd Lieut Jn. Elliott 2nd Lieut W.C. Dickenson. "C" Coy. Captain J. Brunton M.C. Captain J. Rutherford. 2nd Lieut A.E. Clifford 2nd Lieut V.C. Clergyman 2nd Lieut W.E. Baisdell 2nd Lieut G. Thomas. "D" Coy. Captain Graham Lieut J. Sedgwick 2nd Lieut R. Lunnis 2nd Lieut H. Pennington 2nd Lieut F.A. Minin. 2nd Lieut R.C. Alford.	

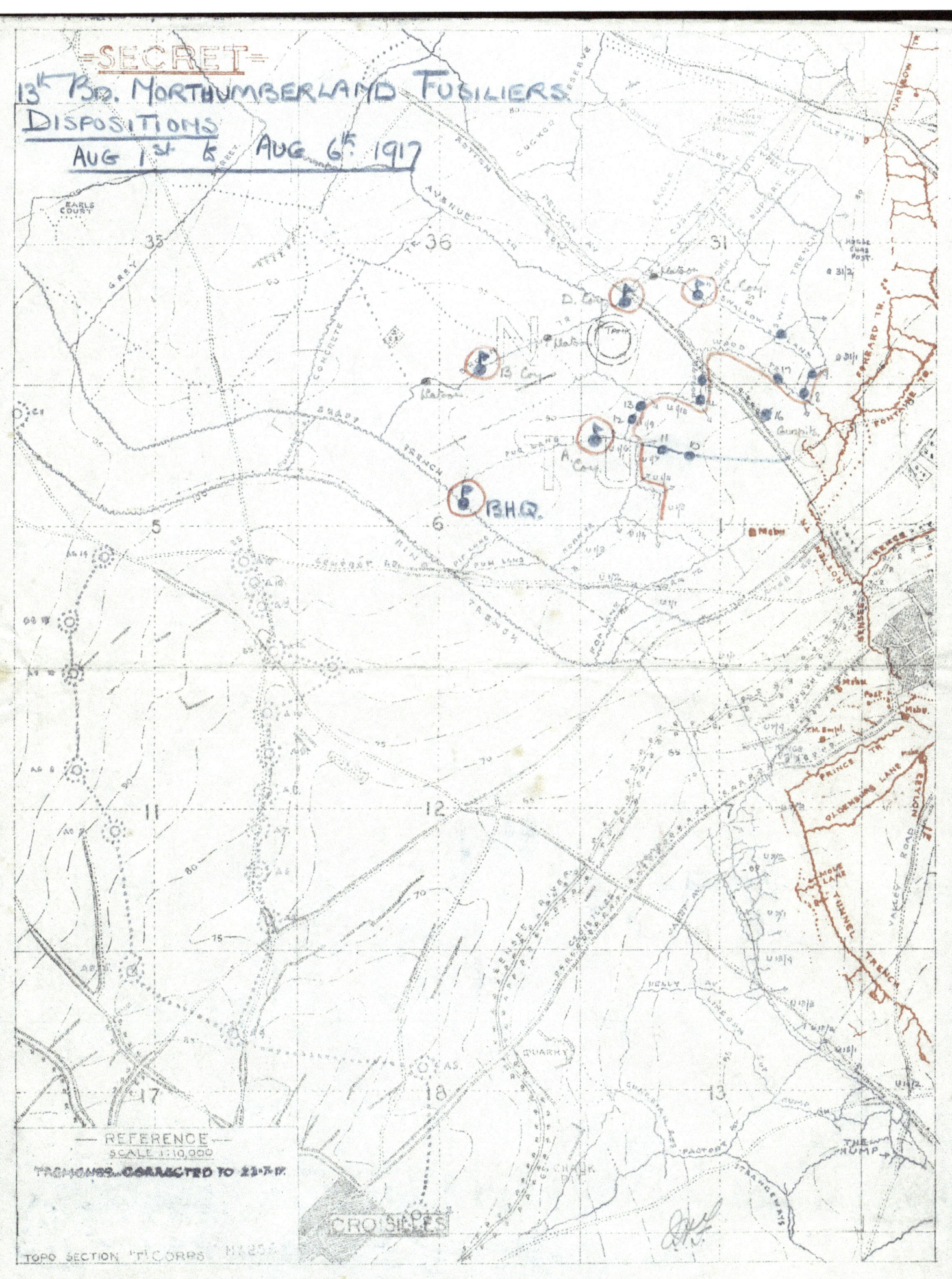

NOMINAL ROLL OF OFFICERS

On Effective Strength

Lt-Col P.H.Stevenson B.S.O.
Major F.J.F.Edlmann D.S.O.
Capt G.White M.C.
Capt J.Brunton M.C.
Capt J.Lockie M.C.
Capt E.W.Shann   (England, War Office)
Capt D.E.Waight
Lieut R.C.Hobson   (Staff)
Lieut W.T.Hindmarch
Lieut J.McKinnon
Lieut G.M.Philip D.S.O. M.C.
Lieut C.N.G.Koch
2/Lt R.C.Alford
2/Lt N.H.Sisterson
2/Lt B.Reading
2/Lt J.O.Byrne
2/Lt G.Sherwood
2/Lt B.A.Briance   T.M.Batty
2/Lt F.A.Jenkyn   (52nd ~~XXX~~ ~~XXX~~)
2/Lt G.H.Bramwell
2/Lt W.C.Dickinson
2/Lt G.H.Williams   (Base)
2/Lt C.Tolkien   (Hosp)
2/Lt A.Urwin
2/Lt W.E.Waistell
2/Lt J.W. Elliott
2/Lt L. Chapman
2/Lt W.S. Hutchinson
2/Lt P.J. Gregory
2/Lt G. Thomas
2/Lt J. Sedgewick
2/Lt W.B. Marsh
2/Lt G.M. Edmonds
2/Lt E. Watson

Not on effective Strength

Major H.W.Gush M.C.   (Attd 1st Lincoln R.)
Lieut W.G.Ferrier-Kerr   (Attd 45th T.M.Batty)
2/Lieut J.O.Durham   (Posted, not yet joined)
2/Lt J.Mowatt   (In Hosp Wounded)

        No of Officers on Effective Strength 34
           do   not on E.S.   4
                                                       ──
                                                       38
                                                       ──

13th (S) Bn Northumberland Fusiliers.

OPERATION ORDER   NO 34.   COPY NO...6...

August 5th.17.

:-:-:-:-:-:-:-:-:-:-:-:

1. The 51st and 50th Divisions are to be transferred to the VI Corps at noon on August 7th 1917.

2. The 151st Inf. Bde will relieve the 62nd Inf. Bde North of the line PUG Avenue - SHAFT Trench to its junction with BROWN Support.
   62nd Inf Bde will relieve 64th Inf Bde as far as the junction of NELLY and BURG Trenches.

3. Commencing at 2.30 a.m. tomorrow Aug 6th "B" Coy will take over posts in PUG AVENUE from 13th Northd Fus. "A" Coy will extend its left to No 3 Post inclusive. "D" Coy will extend from No 3 Post exclusive to the angle of HORNE TRENCH at about U.1.a.35.05. "B" Coy will hold from U.1.a.35.05 to the left of the Brigade Sector where it will link up with the 50th Div.

4. C,B,and D Coys will notify completion of relief by sending the word "WALTER" by wire to H.Q.

5. H.Q. of 62nd T.M.Battery and 62nd M.G.Coy will move to the H.Q. at present occupied by 13th Northd Fus.

6. Seperate instructions have been issued as to taking over Trench Stores.

................Captain.
Adjutant. 13th (s) Battalion.
Northumberland Fusiliers.

Copies.
   No 1 H.Q.
      2 "A"
      3 "B"   Issued at 0.0 p.m.
      4 "C"   by runner.
      5 "D"
      6 13th Northd Fus.

Batt HQ   SECRET
T.6.16.1.2   13th Northumberland Fusiliers   Copy No 1
Ref Sheet   Operation Order No 46   5/8/17
Corps Map 255

I   The 9th Battn Durham Light Infantry will relieve the 13th Battn Northumberland Fusiliers in the Left Sub-Sector (less posts in PUG AVENUE) on August 6th — Relief to be completed by 6 pm except post 16 which will be completed by 11 pm.

II   The 12th Battn Northumberland Fusiliers will relieve the 13th Battn North'd Fus's in the posts in PUG AVENUE — Relief to be completed by 1 pm — Details of Relief will be arranged by Company Commanders concerned.

III   DETAILS:-
(1) "D" Coy 9th D.L.I will relieve "C" Coy 13th North'd Fus's — "C" Coy 13th North'd Fus's will send guides for posts to be at gate in SNIPE TRENCH at 3 pm.
(2) "C" Coy 9th D.L.I will relieve "A" & "D" Coys 13th North'd Fus's. "A" & "D" Coys 13th North'd Fus's will send guides for posts to be at junction

of FIRST AVENUE and SWALLOW LANE - N 36. d 95.65 at 4 p.m.

(3) The 13th Batt'n North'd Fus'rs on relief will move into Brigade Support.

(4) On relief "C" Coy will march by platoons via BUSH TRENCH, PUG LANE to BOYELLES.

(5) On relief "A" Coy will march by platoons to BOYELLES.

(6) On relief "D" Coy will march by platoons via PUG LANE to HIND TRENCH (between FULDNER and FIT LANES)

(7) At 4.30 p.m. "B" Coy will march by platoons and take over posts C 6 to C 10 (both inclusive)

IV All movement East of BOYELLES will be by platoons at 5 minutes interval. Strictest march discipline will be observed and all details from Battalion or Company Headquarters will march in formed bodies under command of an N.C.O.

V Completion of relief will be reported to Battalion Headquarters by the word BEEF.

VII Battalion Headquarters will be at

The Camp Boyelles.

VII Acknowledge.

Issued by Orderly at 7 pm
N°° 1 & 2 Retained
3   A Coy
4   B "
5   C "
6   D "
7   HQ "
8   TO
9   QM.
10 RSM.
11 12th North'd Fus⁰ˢ
12 9th Durham L Inf¹y

O Tippetts
2nd Lieut &
A/Adjutant
13th North'd Fus⁰ˢ

To O.C.
   8th Leicester Regiment
To O/C "B" and "D" Coys

Ref. O.O 68 paragraph III d/8/8/17
"D" Coy will supply 2 guides for "C" Coy
8th Leicester Regt to be at the Rendezvous
at 7.30 p.m.
"B" Coy will supply 2 guides for "B" Coy
8th Leicester Regiment to be at the Rendezvous
at 2 p.m.

                                   W. Leggett
                                   Lieut & A/Adjt
9/8/17   15th North'd Fus'rs

Battⁿ HQ
T.22.d.6.9   13th Northumberland Fus^{rs}   SECRET Copy N° 1
Ref Sheet:-   Operation Order N° 48   8/8/17
51^B S.W.

I. The 110th Infantry Brigade will relieve 62nd Infantry Brigade in the Left Sector of the Divisional Front on August 9th. On relief 62nd Infantry Brigade will be in Divisional Reserve.

II. The 13th Battⁿ Northumberland Fusiliers in Brigade Support, will be relieved by 8th Battalion Leicester Regiment. Relief to be complete by 6 p.m.

III. "A" Coy 13th Northumberland Fusiliers will be relieved by "A" Coy 8th Battⁿ Leicester Regiment.
"B" Company 13th North'd Fusiliers will be relieved by "B" Company 8th Battⁿ Leicester Reg^t.
"C" Company 13th North'd Fusiliers will be relieved by "D" Coy 8th Battⁿ Leicester Reg^t.
"D" Company 13th North'd Fusiliers will be relieved by "C" Company 8th Battⁿ Leicester Reg^t.
"B" and "D" Coys 13th North'd Fusiliers will send platoon guides to be at Cross Roads T.21.d.55.80 at 2 p.m.

IV. On relief the 13th Battⁿ North'd Fusiliers will proceed to "A" Camp, Moyenneville.

V. The Transport Officer will make arrangements to have requisite transport for Lewis Guns, Boxes etc at the Red Flag (B & D Coys) and at the Cross Roads

T 33. D.I.Y (A & C Companies) at 3.30 pm

VI Acknowledge.

Copies Nos 1 & 2 Retained
Copy No 3 A Coy
" 4 B "
5 C "
6 D "
7 HQ "
8 TO "
9 QM "
10 RSM "
11 8th Leicester Regt
12 62nd Infy Bde

W. Leggett
2nd Lieut & A/Adjt
13th Northumberland Fus.rs

Batt HQ
Boyelles

Ref. Sheet
51B S.W.

13th Northumberland Fusiliers
Operation Order No 47

SECRET
Copy No 1

7.3.17

I. The 13th Batt'n Northumberland Fusiliers (less 2 Companies) will relieve 10th Batt'n King's Own Yorkshire Light Infantry (less two Companies) in Brigade Support this evening.

II. "A" Comp'y 13th North'd Fus'rs will relieve 1 Coy K.O.Y.L.I. in the Quarry T.18.b. at 7 pm. Guides will be at the Factory T.24.a.65.55 at 6.30 pm.

"B" Comp'y 13th North'd Fusiliers will relieve 1 Coy K.O.Y.L.I. in the Sunken Road T.23.a. at 6.30 pm.

"HQ" Company will move off at 6.30 pm.

III. All movement east of BOYELLES will be by platoons at 5 minutes interval. Strictest march discipline will be observed and all details from Battalion or Company Headquarters will march in formed bodies under command of an N.C.O.

IV. Completion of relief will be reported by word "BULLY".

V. Reports after 8 pm to Batt'n Headquarters at T.22.d.6.9.

VI. Acknowledge.

Issued by Orderly at 1.30 pm.

No 1 & 2 Retained
    3   "A" Coy
    4   "B"
    5   "C"
    6   "D"
    7   H.Q.
    8   T.O.
    9   Q.M.
   10   R.S.M.
   11   10th K.O.Y.L.I.
   12   62nd Inf'y Bde.

D.K. Leggett.

2nd Lieut. & Adjt.
13th North'd Fusiliers

WAR DIARY or INTELLIGENCE SUMMARY

Army Form C. 2118.

12/13th North Fus

Vol 2 5

Place	Date 1917.	Hour	Summary of Events and Information	Remarks and references to Appendices
BERNEVILLE	Sept 1.		The 12/13 Battn Northumberland Fusiliers in Rest billets in the XVIIth Corps Area; a draft of 79 O.R. arrived from the 31st I.B.D. Training carried out in the new method of attack, and all anti gas appliances tested and gas drill practiced constantly.	Map of the ARRAS 1/40,000
	2.		34 O.R. arrived as a Reinforcement for the 31st I.B.D. Battalion bearing and reorganising carried out.	
	3.		2 Lt A.F. WOODS and 2 Lt T. WILKINSON transferred to the 8th Battalion Northumberland Fusiliers.	
	4-7		The 62nd Bde held an assault at Arms at DAINVILLE, in which the 12/13 Battn was highly successful, securing 8 first places and 12 second places in a total of 22 events.	
	8.		A Reinforcement of 9 O.R. arrived from the 31st I.B.D.	
	10.			
	13th		The Battalion marched from BERNEVILLE to SAVY and entrained there at 8 p.m. travelling via ST POL	
	16.		AIRE and HAZEBOUK, CAESTRE was reached at 7AM where the Battalion detrained and marched into billets in the PRADELLES area. Battalion Headquarters were located in PRADELLES whilst A and C Coys in farms near that village; B and D Coys were in farms near BORRE, where 62nd Bde HQrs were situated.	map HAZEBROUK 5 A 1/100,000
	17.		A draft of 16 other ranks joined the Battalion from the 31st I.B.D. The Billets were found to be good, although scattered and the attitude of the inhabitants unusually friendly. Weather very fine and warm. The 21st Division now under orders of the 10th Corps.	
PRADELLES	18.		A draft of 7 O.R. joined the Battalion from 31st I.B.D. The Battalion continued its training, special attention being paid to tactical schemes from James Officers NCOs, to fit them for the new warfare occasioned by the altered German tactics of holding isolated shell holes instead of a trench line.	

WAR DIARY
or
INTELLIGENCE SUMMARY

Army Form C. 2118.

(Erase heading not required.)

Place	Date 1917	Hour	Summary of Events and Information	Remarks and references to Appendices
PRADELLES	Sept 19		A few 15 inch naval shells fired by the enemy fell near D Coys billets doing no damage; they were probably intended for the railway station at HAZEBROUCK about ¾ mile distant, but were fired at a range of over 20 miles were carried wide by the breeze.	Map HAZEBROUCK 5A 1 100,000
	20		2 Lt Edmonds and 40 O.R of A Coy detailed for duty on burial tramways in the DICKEBUSCH area.	
	21-22		Battalion remained at PRADELLES training; weather continued very fine.	
	23		Battalion marched from PRADELLES via FLETRE to LE ROUKLOSHILLE, a distance of about 4 miles and went into farm billets in and around that area. Bde Hd qrs at LE ROUKLOSHILLE. Brind Hdqs METEREN.	
LE ROUKLOSHILLE			2 Lt J. RIDLEY and 10 O.R arrived from the 31st I.B.D	
	24		The Battalion continued training in the new area.	
	25		Two platoons of B Coy detached for duty on Corps dumps & tramways in the DICKEBUSCH AREA. 2 Lt E.ASTBURY joined the Battalion from 31st I.B.D.	
	26.27.		Battalion continued training in the LE ROUKLOSHILLE AREA.	
	28.		Battalion marched from LE ROUKLOSHILLE to ARRAGON camp 1 mile west of WESTOUTRE. The day was very hot, but no men fell out. Camp was reached at 2.30 pm.	
WESTOUTRE	29. -30.		Very fine hot weather, hostile aeroplanes very active at night, a large numbers of bombs were dropped, but none in the immediate vicinity of the camp. The Battalion Lewis guns engaged the hostile aircraft at intervals during the night.	

Millman Major p ltCol

Comdg 12/13 Batt: Middx Regt

WAR DIARY or INTELLIGENCE SUMMARY

Army Form C. 2118.

62/31 12/13th North Fusiliers Vol 26

Place	Date	Hour	Summary of Events and Information	Remarks and references to Appendices
WESTOUTRE	1917 Oct 1st		The Battalion (12/13 North'd Fusiliers) marched out of ARRAGON camp WESTOUTRE to a bivouac between RIDGE and SCOTTISH WOODS – immediately south of DICKEBUSCH LAKE, a march which was detailed at WESTOUTRE and marched under MAJOR E. DUMMIN DSO. to MICROMBIDGEE CAMP at LA CLYTTE.	Ref Map: Sheet 28 Edition 3 1/40,000
	Oct 2		There was considerable bombing near the Battalion bivouac, but no damage was done to Battalion lines. The Battalion marched from the bivouac at SCOTTISH WOOD to DUNBRECK LAKE at 4 p.m; teas were taken on the south side of the lake; some shelling was experienced here. At dusk the Battalion moved up into Bde support – the 62nd Bde taking over from the 110th Inf Bde. The Battn. Transport remained at SCOTTISH WOOD (N.5.A)	
	Oct 3.		The 3/4 Battn. QUEENS Royal West Surrey Regt held the Bdy front line, the 12th being on the left of the front and the 64th Bde on the right of the 11th Bde in Divisional Reserve. The Bde Frontage held by the Royal West Surrey Regt extended from J.10.D.2.5. to J.11.C.40.55. The 12/13 North'd Fusiliers & the 10th Northd Yorkshire regt were in support Batts, respectively, the 12/13 North'd Fusiliers having 2 Coys (C & D Coys) in trenches on the Eastern edge of GLENCORSE WOOD and A & B Coys & Battn. H.Qrs. in the tunnel at CLAPHAM JUNCTION (J.13D.7.8.). The Batt. carried on the normal work all day, there was occasional heavy shell fire, but casualties were not heavy. 62nd Bde H.Qrs. were in SANCTUARY WOOD at J.13.C.65.10.	
	Oct 4.		The 21st Division was ordered to attack the line J.11.C.55.05 – J.11.d.2.3 – J.12.a.1.5. in conjunction with the 5th Division on the right and 7th Division on the left and "to form a defensive flank facing South south-east and East with a view to protecting the Southern flank of the attacking troops on the North" (the remainder of the Second army, including the Anzac Corps) "and obtaining observation of the REUTELBEEK VALLEY and the spur	3-a (1)

WAR DIARY or INTELLIGENCE SUMMARY

Army Form C. 2118.

Place	Date	Hour	Summary of Events and Information	Remarks and references to Appendices
POLYGON WOOD (nr. ZONNEBEKE)	Oct 4		Morning S.E. to BECELAIRE. The 62nd Bde attacked on the left of the Divisional front, the 64th Bde on the right and Reserve Bde were in Divisional Reserve. The 62nd Bde had as 1st objective the Road from J.11.c.60.55 to J.11.a.85.30. For this the 3/4 QUEENS were detailed, the second objective was the line J.11.d.65.75 – J.11.b.95.15 – J.12.a.15., this was to be carried by the 12/13 Nor'd Fusiliers on the right and 10" Batt. Yorkshire Regt on the left; the 1st Batt. LINCOLNSHIRE REGT being in Bde Reserve. At 2 A.M. on the morning of Oct 4th C and D Coys moved forward to their assembly position immediately in rear of the jumping-off position of the 3/4 "QUEENS". A & B Coys followed by Batt. Hdqrs moved from CLAPHAM JUNCTION at the same time. Between GLENCORSE WOOD and POLYGON WOOD a hostile barrage was encountered, but the Coys pushed on & suffered comparatively few casualties. At about 5.20 A.M the Battn. had formed up in its position for the assault as follows: D. Coy on the right, C. Coy on the left, A Coy supporting D Coy and B Coy supporting C Coy. Batt. Hdqrs immediately in rear of B Coy. The Coys were formed of three platoons & were formed up each on a one platoon front echeloned in depth. The 10th Batt. the YORKSHIRE REGT having been caught in a hostile barrage the 1st Batt. LINCOLNSHIRE REGT came up on the left of the 12/13 Batt. Nor'thd Fusiliers. At 3.00 (6 A.M.) the Battn. moved forward to the attack (the final objective of the Battn. being a line drawn from the SOUTHERN END of JUDGE COPSE on the right to JUDGE COTT on the left); moving forward close behind	Sheet 28. Edition 3. 1/40.000

Army Form C. 2118.

WAR DIARY
or
INTELLIGENCE SUMMARY
(Erase heading not required.)

Instructions regarding War Diaries and Intelligence Summaries are contained in F. S. Regs., Part II. and the Staff Manual respectively. Title Pages will be prepared in manuscript.

Place	Date	Hour	Summary of Events and Information	Remarks and references to Appendices
Near REUTEL	Oct 4th	6 A.M.	The 3/4 QUEEN'S ROYAL WEST SURREYS the first opposition encountered by the Battalion was from the still held of the enemy original frontline where some of the enemy officers & have been harassed men by the leading Battalion, & several casualties were suffered. After crossing JUNIPER TRENCH the Battalion came under fire from both flanks; on the right a strong point which was not being attended to by any troops opened fire & caused trouble, 2Lt EDMONDS at moved up the Altn on the right flank of the Baltn and attacked & captured this strong point, taking between 30 and 40 prisoners, a party of the K.O.Y.L.I. (64th Bde) who came up shortly afterwards were left at this strong point as a garrison. A Coy moving on half left resumed its position in support of D Coy. Meanwhile on the left flank C and B Coys suffered casualties from a strong point near JUNIPER TRENCH (about J.10.D.6.8.) near junction of 12/13 Northd Fusiliers with the right flank of 1st LINCOLN Regt; at conjunction with 14(?) 1st Div C/m Regt this strong point was captured. Continuing the advance the Battalion became somewhat scattered owing to the boggy nature of the ground chiefly on the left flank; heavy rifle & M.G. fire was now directed against the Baltn from the opposite ridge and a strong point near JUDEE TRENCH (about J.11.C.7.3), heavy casualties were suffered here. One strong point at J.11.C.7.8 was captured by B Coy, rifle grenades being used first with good effect. Meanwhile heavy machine gun fire continued to come from the front & right flank & many casualties occurred. Lt Col DIX M.C. now reorganised the O/. 2 half Baltn & leading on B Coy unto the frontline to strengthen E Coy was himself killed whilst leading. He now arriving men of these two Coys together their first objective, Capt RIDDELL, who was already wounded took command but would it impossible to advance further owing to the heavy fire & the weakness	Sheet 28 Edition 3. 1/40,000

WAR DIARY or INTELLIGENCE SUMMARY

Army Form C. 2118.

Place	Date	Hour	Summary of Events and Information	Remarks and references to Appendices
REUTEL	Oct 4 1917		and gave orders to consolidate the first objective, along the line of what the 12/13 Mid'd'x Fusiliers & 1 Batt. LINCOLNSHIRE were now mixed with the men of the 3/4 QUEENS. At this juncture Capt. RIDDELL was severely wounded & the command of the Batt. passed to Lieut. McKINNON, the LEWIS GUN officer, all other officers (& him [?]) having become casualties; one officer who now took each Coy namely 2Lt EDMONDS in command of A Coy, 2nd JACKSON of B Coy, 2nd CHERRYMAN of C Coy, and 2nd HUTCHINSON of D Coy. Before the barrage moved on D Coy found it necessary to attack a strong point at J.11.e.65.60 on the right of the Batt front which was causing trouble, a large number of the enemy were killed & this point and three machine guns captured.	sheet 28 Edition 3. 1/40,000
		7.40 AM	At zero plus 100 minutes the barrage moved on according to plan (7.40 AM) & a line of the captured the final objective & the 12/13 Mid'd'x Fusiliers on the right & 1 Batt. LINCOLNSHIRE Regt. pushed on towards their respective objectives still under the heavy machine gun & shell fire directed from the ridge opposite. Having reached a front about 250 yds short of the final objective the Batt. dug in, in line with the 1 Batt. LINCOLN'S for the left & connecting up & linking up with the 9 Batt. K.O.Y.L.I. There was at once formed on the right by A Coy who attained touch with the 9 Batt. K.O.Y.L.I. Consolidation was satisfactorily completed by dusk and A Coy withdrew into close support in half trench from our original front line. No counter attacks developed against the Batt. front, but heavy barrage fire constantly fell on the Batt. owing to S.O.S. signals sent up by neighbouring units.	
	Oct 5		Early in the morning Capt. BRUNTON, M.C. took charge of the Batt. & remained in command until the	

WAR DIARY
or
INTELLIGENCE SUMMARY

Army Form C. 2118.

Place	Date	Hour	Summary of Events and Information	Remarks and references to Appendices
NEAR REUTEL	Oct 5th		6th Batt. LEICESTERSHIRE REGT. relieved the 1st Batt. LINCOLNSHIRE REGT. 4/5/10/15 Notified parties on the evening of Oct 5th. Lt. McKINNON marched the Batt. out to the BUND at ZILLEBEKE LAKE, Capt. BRUNTON remaining behind to point out the position to the new Battalion, Capt. Brunton was severely wounded on the evening of Oct 6th	Sheet 28 Edition 3. 1/40,000.
	Oct 6th		The Battalion arrived at ZILLEBEKE LAKE at 3 AM & went into dugouts. The casualties suffered were:- Officers killed 7 – Lt. Col. S.H. DIX M.C., Lt. FEGETTER, Lt. LOWTH, 2/Lt. WAISTELL, 2/Lt. LUMMIS, 2/Lt. GREGORY and 2/Lt. LETHBRIDGE, wounded 13 – Capt. OAKSHOTT, Capt. RIDDELL, Capt. HERBERT, Capt. GRAHAM, Capt. GRIFFIN M.C. R.A.M.C. (remained at duty), Lt. PHILIP D.S.O. M.C., Lt. BRAMWELL, Lt. DICKENSON, Lt. ALFORD, 2/Lt. THOMAS, 2/Lt. KAWIN wounded. Capt. BRUNTON AE & Lt. CLIFFORD. The Officer in charge carrying party; 4 O.R. killed, 326 O.R. wounded. At 9 pm the Batt. moved from ZILLEBERT LAKE to SCOTTISH WOOD.	
	Oct 7th		At 2 pm the Batt. moved from SCOTTISH WOOD. The nucleus party located; Major J.J. EDIMANN D.S.O. assumed command of the Battalion, the following Officers of the nucleus party assumed command of companies, Capt. WAIGHT of A Coy., Lt. BYRNE of B Coy, Capt. ROTHERFORD of C Coy, Lt. DEEMING of D Coy. During the period of active operations 2nd Lt. R.M. COMLEY arrived from 3rd I.B.D. on Oct 2nd and Lt. F.L. SMART on Oct 4 together with 4 O.R. The Batt. marched at 2.30 pm to OUDERDOM and entrained there, detrained at 11 pm at EBLINGHEM and marched into billets at LA BELLE HOTESSE, transport proceeded by road.	HAZEBROUCK 5.A. 1/100,000
LA BELLE HOTESSE.	Oct 8 Oct 9. Oct 10.		The Batt. reorganised at LA BELLE HOTESSE, Coys were reformed from 3 to 2 platoons each and LEWIS GUN teams made up to strength (16 teams, each of 1 N.C.O and 6).	

WAR DIARY
or
INTELLIGENCE SUMMARY

(Erase heading not required.)

Army Form C. 2118.

Place	Date	Hour	Summary of Events and Information	Remarks and references to Appendices
YPRES	1917 Oct 11th		The Battalion moved by motor bus to a camp ¾ mile N.W. of YPRES, and came under the orders of the 2nd ANZAC Corps for work on LIGHT Rlys under the 2nd Canadian Rly Battalion.	sheet 28 Zillebeke 3. 1/40,000
	11-18		The Battalion worked daily on the light railway between ST JEAN and the Front Line. The camp was frequently bombed by Fleets of GOTHA airplanes, but only one bomb caused casualties, one bomb which fell on 18th casualty casualties to 13.O.R.	
	Oct 18		At 3.30pm Battalion moved by motor lorry to MICMAC camp between MALLEDAST and OVERDOM and there came under orders of the 110th Bde 2nd Loks command division.	
	19-21		The Battn. remained in MICMAC camp, teaming and reorganising; bombs were dropped nightly by hostile aircraft but no damage caused; on Oct 18th 2 Lt G. Jackson arrived as a reinforcement. on Oct 21st 2 Lts J. RICHARDSON, M.A. THOMPSON, W. BRIGHAM, E.R.M. GREENFIELD, E.S. MILNE and G.H.R. DOLMAN reported for duty together with 98 O.Rs from 3rd & 1st B.D.	
	Oct 21		The Battalion marched from MICMAC camp to SCOTTISH WOOD. The battalion was heavily bombed at 5.30pm by airplanes near CONFUSION CORNER, but escaped with one casualty. The Batth rested in camp at SCOTTISH WOOD.	
	Oct 22 Oct 23 " 24		The Batth marched up the ZILLEBEKE BUND and went into Bde reserve, the 1st LINCOLNS being in the support and the 10th Batth N. Yorkshire Regt and 3/4 Batth The QUEEN'S holding the Bde Front line, the Bde HQrs were in MOOSE CRATERS; the Bde on left subsector of 21st Divisional Front, 64th Bde on right.	
	Oct 25		The night on the 110th Bde in support. MAJOR EDMANN, Capt McKinnon & Lt KOCH went up to the Headquarters of the Queen Royal West Surrey Regt to reconnoitre the route, on anxious return that Batth, on the return journey MAJOR EDMANN was	

WAR DIARY
or
INTELLIGENCE SUMMARY
(Erase heading not required.)

Army Form C. 2118.

Place	Date	Hour	Summary of Events and Information	Remarks and references to Appendices
ZILLEBEKE	Oct 26		wounded but returned to the Battalion. 2/Lt H.T. GREENE arrived as a reinforcement.	Strat 28 Platoon 3,
	Oct 26.	5.40 AM	At 5.40 AM the Division on the night of the IX Corps front attacked the 5th Division attacked POLDERHOEK CHATEAU, the 7th Division GHELUVELT; no attack was made by 21st Division.	40,000 and BECELAERE
		2.30 PM	At 2.30 pm the 12/13 Northd Fusiliers marched by platoons to HOOGE CRATER where guides of the 3/4 Queens conducted them up to the front line. Lt Col N.G. KOCH accompanied Major EDMANN an intelligence officer & Capt J. McKINNON Asst Adj, Capt S. WHITE M.C. 2nd Second-in-Command remained with the transport. Confusedly little shelling was encountered on the march up the duck boarded HELLE'S track, but Capt RUTHERFORD was wounded by a shell together with eleven other ranks while C Coy was relieving the right Coy of the 3/4 QUEENS. The relief was completed by 7.25 pm and the position then was; B Coy Hdqrs at HOOGE CRATER; 1/c Battn LINCOLNSHIRE REGT on right; B Coy astride and 11/13 Battn Nthd Fusiliers in the left subsector; with right at flank at J.6.B.35.05 and left flank at J.5.B.5.5. Two Coys in the front line were, on the right C Coy, on the left B Coy; A Coy in position for counter attack at J.5. central. A Coy; Coy in support D Coy at from J.4.D.9.5 to J.4.D.7.7. Battn Hdqrs were at J.5.C.10.75. On the left the Battn was in touch will the 23rd Battn AUSTRALIAN INFTY 7th Bde, 2 Division, 1st ANZAC.	Reinforcements at 26. 2/Lt G.W. LACEY & 3.O.R. from 3rd I.B.D. at 27 LT H.P. ADAMS & 2.O.I.R. from 31 I.B.D.
GOOBEZEGHOCK	Oct 27		The enemy's artillery was very active. Heavy barrage fell behind our front line between 4 and 6 A.M. no infantry action followed, throughout the day there was intermittent shelling.	
	Oct 28		During heavy shelling at stand to in the morning, 2/Lt E.S. MILNE was killed in a front line patrol. Left Coy. Hostile aircraft very active, flying low over front line, and without interference by our own	

Army Form C. 2118.

WAR DIARY
or
INTELLIGENCE SUMMARY
(Erase heading not required.)

Instructions regarding War Diaries and Intelligence Summaries are contained in F. S. Regs., Part II and the Staff Manual respectively. Title Pages will be prepared in manuscript.

Place	Date	Hour	Summary of Events and Information	Remarks and references to Appendices
NOORDEMDHOEK	Oct 28		aircraft, the routine offensive to trouble the low flying hostile airplanes is most noticeable; enemy's aircraft were engaged with LEWIS GUNS and VICKERS GUNS	BECELAERE 1/10,000
	Oct 29		The 2nd Army Artillery opened a heavy practice barrage at 5.40AM, the hostile retaliating barrage being also heavy and 12 casualties were suffered from it. Back areas were also heavily shelled, during which BRIGADIER GENERAL C.S. RAWLING C.M.G. C.I.E. commanding the 62nd Inf/Y Bde was killed at HOOGE CRATER; General RAWLING had commanded this Bde with great success since June 1916. Inter Coy reliefs were carried out without casualties at dusk; D Coy relieved C Coy in the right Coy area, A Coy replaced B Coy in left Coy area. Hostile shelling very severe, owing to feint attack being made by means of a creeping barrage towards BECELAERE by the supporting Artillery (3rd AUSTRALIAN F.A. Bde and 113 Army F.A. Bde). Some casualties were suffered by hostile repentive and supporting corps the weather which had been exceptionally fine nine at 25 became overcast and rainy. Most of the AUSTRALIANS, the CANADIANS attacked PASSCHENDAEL.	
	Oct 30		The day was exceptionally quiet, but in the evening the enemy put up a heavy barrage of gas well which seriously interfered with the incoming relief, the 15th Batln DURHAM LIGHT INF'Y suffering heavy casualties before effecting the relief of the 12/13 Batln NorthD Fusilrs; the relief was completed at 10.15 p.m. and before lunch to ZILLEBEKE BUND without casualties. The 64th Bde relieved the NorthumberLand Fusiliers marched back to ZILLEBEKE BUND without casualties. The 62nd Bde and the relief went into Divisional reserve.	Oct 31st 2 Lt G. NOBLE & 3.0.R arrived from 31st I.B.D.
	Oct 31			

J.M. Bollman Major
Comdg 12/13 Batln NorthD Fusiliers

SECRET

Ref. Map
Sheet 28
Belgium & France
GHELUVELT 1/10000

12/13th BN NORTHUMBERLAND FUSILIERS

OPERATION ORDER NO.9

Copy No... 10...
4.10.17

1. (a) The Second Army will attack on a day to be notified later against the high ground REUTEL - NOORDEMDHOEK - MOLENAARELSTHOEK - NIEUWE MODEN.

   (b) The 5th Division will attack on the right of the 21st Division - objective, the line J.12.d.65.95 - J.10.d.8.6 - J.17.a.8.8 - J.11.c.55.05.

   (c) The 7th Division will attack on the left of the 21st Division - objective, the line J.12.a.1.5 - J.6.c.35.20 - J.6.b.7.0 - J.5.b.30.15.

   (d) The 19th Reserve Division, lately arrived from RUSSIA is at present believed to be holding the line to be attacked by the 21st Division. Deserters state many men of this Division are quite ready to desert.

2. The objective of the 21st Division is the line J.11.c.55.05 - J.11.d.2.3 - J.11.d.65.75 - J.11.b.95.15 - J.12.a.1.5. The duty of the 21st Division is to form a defensive flank facing South south-east, and East, with a view to protecting the Southern flank of the attacking troops on the North, and obtaining observation of the REUTELBEEK Valley and the spur running S.E. to BECELAIRE.

3. The 64th Infantry Brigade on the right and the 62nd Inf. Bde. on the left will carry out the attack. 110th Inf. Bde. will be in Divisional Reserve.

4. <u>1st Objective</u> - Road from J.11.c.60.55 to J.11.a.85.30.

   <u>2nd Objective</u> - Line J.11.d.65.75 - J.11.b.95.15 - J.12.a.1.5.

5. (a) The attack and capture of the 1st Objective will be carried out by the 3/4th "The Queens" (R.W.S.) Reg.

   (b) The attack and capture of the 2nd Objective will be carried out by the 12/13th Northumberland Fusrs. on the right and 10th York Reg. on the left.

   (c) The 1st Lincoln Regt. will be in Brigade Reserve.

6. Boundaries will be as follows:-

   <u>Brigade Boundary</u> - J.10.d.8.6 - J.11.c.40.55
   J.11.d.2.7 - J.11.d.65.75

   <u>Northern Divl Boundary</u> - J.10.b.3.0 - J.11.a.35.20
   J.12.a.1.5.

   <u>Dividing line between</u> - J.10.d.85.75 - J.11.c.55.90
   <u>12/13th Northd Fus & 10 York R.</u> J.11.b.90.10.

- 1 -

- 2 -

7. The Battn will attack on a 2 Coy front, each Coy on a Platoon Front, "D" Coy on the right and "C" on the left of the front line, "A" on the right and "B" on the left in Support.

8. At ZERO minus sixty minutes "D" and "C" Coys will form up in rear 3/4th "The Queens" (R.W.S.) Reg. keeping as close to them as possible.

At ZERO minus sixty minutes "A" and "B" Coys will form up at a spot to be notified later, approximately 400 yards in rear of the 3/4th "The Queens" (R.W.S.) Reg. jumping off point.

At Zero "D" and "C" Coys will advance with the 3/4th "The Queens" (R.W.S.) Reg. until 150 yards before "The Queens" objective when they will halt.

On the objective being taken "C" and "D" Coys will go through "The Queens" up to the Barrage.

At ZERO plus one hundred minutes the barrage will move and advance at the rate of 100 yards in eight minutes until the final objective has been reached, where the right of the Battalion will rest on the Southern end of JUDGE COPSE and the left on JUDGE COTT.

At ZERO plus 40 "A" and "B" Coys will advance in conjunction with "A" and "C" Coys 10th York Reg. They will pass through "The Queens" and close up behind "D" and "C" Coys.

"A" Coy will then take up its position on the right of the line. "B" Coy in close support.

On the barrage advancing the line will be:-
"A", "D" and "C" Coys front line.
"B" Coy in support.

"B" Coy will correct its distance as the advance proceeds and will halt 250 yards before reaching Objective at the point about J.11.d.CC.40.

The final objective having been taken Posts will be pushed forward as far as possible down the slope to the valley and remain there to break up any counter attack.

On the position being consolidated "D" Coy will withdraw to J.11.d.80.00 and relieve "B" Coy. On relief "B" Coy will withdraw to JUDGE TRENCH.

9. "Battn H.Q. will be with Reserve Company until after advance from JUDGE TRENCH when it will remain there. On arrival at JUDGE TRENCH the Lewis Gun Officer will see that 2 Lewis Guns are left there, with Battn H.Q. the remaining spare guns proceeding with "B" Coy.

10. It is to be understood by all ranks that should the front line be driven in JUDGE TRENCH will be held at all costs.

After the line has been consolidated it will be held lightly and counter-attack Platoons will be withdrawn about 80 yards and keep in close Support.

11. Counter-attack
In the event of a Counter-attack being launched by the enemy after the line has been consolidated O.C. "D" Coy will move up without waiting orders but at the same time reporting his action to O.C. "B" Coy who will immediately move up and take up the position vacated by "D" Coy, reporting his action to O.C. 3/4th "The Queens" (R.W.S.) Reg.

It must be clearly understood that all ground taken must be held at all costs.

"3."

12. The word "RETIRE"

   This word is never to be used in the 21st Division. Summary action is to be taken against any person heard using it.

13. Regimental Aid Post is at J.10.a.3.3.

14. Brigade H.Q. will be at J.16.c.65.10.

15. These Orders are to be destroyed before going into attack.

16. Acknowledge.

T A Oakshott
Captain.
A/Adjutant 12/13th Northumberland Fusiliers

ISSUED BY ORDERLY
at 9.30.p.m

```
Copies No   1   62nd Inf Bde.
            2   64th   "    "
            3   10th Yorks R.
            4   A Coy
            5   B  "
            6   C  "
            7   D  "
            8   R.S.M.
            9   O.M.
           10   2nd in Command
           11   T.O.
           12   Files.
```

SECRET
Copy No. 1.
18.10.17

12/13th NORTHUMBERLAND FUSILIERS
OPERATION ORDER No 13

Ref. Map
Sheet 28 1/40000

xx   Orders for today's move are cancelled and the following substituted.

1.   The Battalion will be relieved by 18th Liverpool Regiment today and will parade at 3.30 p.m in Marching Order, blankets on packs and Great Coat in pack.

   Lorries to convey the Battalion to MICMAC CAMP H.31.d (instead of WESTOUTRE AREA) will be on road between ASYLUM and KRUISSTRAAT at 4.30 p.m.
   ROUTE. VLAMERTINGHE-OUDERDOM-MICMAC.
   Transport will move by the same route parading at 3 p.m under the Transport Officer.

2.   Officers Valises etc will be at the Q.M. Stores by 2 p.m
   Mess Boxes and Orderly Room Boxes will be at the Orderly Room by 2 p.m
   One Lorry will be at the Orderly Room by 3 p.m to collect surplus blankets etc, One N.C.O. per Coy i/c and one Sick man per Coy will travel with the Lorry.

3.   Dinners will be served at 1 p.m today.
   Teas will be issued at MICMAC Camp, no rations or camp kettles will be carried on the men.

4.   The A/Q.M. will hand over all Tentage, tools etc to the advanced party of the incoming Battalion and obtain a receipt for same.

                                   C. White
                              .... Captain.
                         Adjutant 12/13th Northumberland Fusiliers

ISSUED by Orderly at 11.30 a.m
   Copy No 1 File
          2 C.O.
          3 110th Inf Bde.
          4 A. Coy
          5 B "
          6 C "
          7 D "
          8 R.S.M.
          9 Q.M.
         10 A/SSM H.Q.
         11 Transport Officer.

SECRET.

C.O., 12/13th North Fus.
Goldfish Chateau.

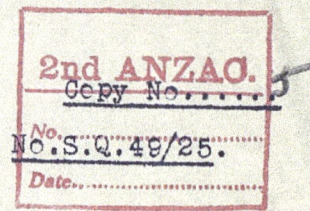
2nd ANZAC.
Copy No.......
No. S.Q. 49/25.
Date........

MOVE ORDER - Ref: Map Sh.28. 1/40,000

The three Battalions of the 21st DIVISION at work in this Area will be relieved on the afternoon of the 18th inst. as follows :-

    1st LINCOLNS will be relieved by 1st SHERWOOD FORESTERS.
    15th DURHAMS will be relieved by 17th MANCHESTERS.
    12/13 NORTHUMBERLAND FUS: will be relieved by 18th LIVERPOOLS.

Battalions will move by lorries embussing on road between ASYLUM and KRUISSTRAAT at 4-30 p.m. on 18th inst. Route, VLAMERTINGHE - OUDERDOM - MICMAC - WESTOUTRE. Transport will move by same route. Supply wagons will be handed over to Fifth Division train on 18th inst. Advance parties of relieving Battalions will arrive about noon on the 18th to take over camps and will arrange for guides to meet their Battalions at debussing point, to guide Battalions to their camps.

Rations for consumption on the 19th will be carried.

Work will continue on the morning of the 18th as usual.

                                         Serjeant

Headquarters,
  17th October, 1917.
DISTRIBUTION -
  1. "G"
  2. "Q"
  3. 1st Lincolns.
  4. 15th Durhams.
  5. 12/13 North.Fus.
  6. 8th Division
  7. 30th Division.
  8. N.Z. Divn.
  9. A.P.M.
10. Canadian Corps.
11. Area Comdt. YPRES N.
12.)
13.)
14.) Spares.
15.)

Lieut.-Colonel,
D.A.Q.M.G.
2nd ANZAC Corps.

Relief Orders No 2   25.10.17
              by
Major H.C. Cannon, M.C., OXEN

1. **Relief.** The Battalion will be relieved in the line by B.E.A.R. on the night 26th–27th Oct.
"C" Coy BEAR will relieve "B" Coy OXEN
"B" Coy BEAR will relieve "D" Coy OXEN
"A" "   "   "   "   "C" "   "
"D" "   "   "   "   "A" "   "

2. **Guides.** Four guides per Coy. & two from HQ under 2/Lt. Shepherd will meet BEAR at HOOGE CRATER at 4 p.m., 26th inst. and will lead relieving Batt. in by HELLES TRACK in the following order:— H.Q. C Coy — "B" Coy — A Coy. & "D" Coy.

3. **Advance Party.** One officer & two runners per Coy of BEAR will attend at B.H.Q. on the evening of the 25th inst., & will be guided thence to their respective Coys. O.C. Coys. will ensure that the runners of "BEAR" take every available opportunity of reconnoitring the route to B.H.Q.

4. **Reserve Positions.** On completion of relief "A" & "C" Coys. will proceed to RAILWAY DUGOUTS I.21.d.4.6. whilst "B" & "D" Coys. proceed to dug-outs in the BUND, the West bank of

2.
ZILLEBEKE I. 21.6.15.

- Carrier Pigeons (contd.)

5. Completion of Relief. O.C. Coys. will report completion of relief to B.H.Q. by runner. There must be no delay in doing this. Code word for relief SMITH.

6. Move. On completion of relief Coys will proceed independently to new quarters in no larger or smaller bodies than 1 platoon.

7. Move. O.C. Coys are reminded that the relief must be carried out with all possible speed further to ensure the Battalion missing hostile barrages. All their men must be ready to move away by 5 p.m.

8. Handing Over. All forks, maps, tapes, pigeons, periscopes, bombs, rifle grenades must be handed over to incoming unit.

9. Acknowledgement. Acknowledge.

A.B.Ord
Lieut.
A/Adjt.

```
                19/13th NORTHUMBERLAND FUSILIERS          SECRET
                    OPERATION ORDER No 15               Copy No. 4.
                                                         25.10.17.
Ref Maps:
  Sheet 28.
```

1.   The Battalion will relieve 3/4th QUEENS (RWS) REGT
        in the Left Sub-Sector tomorrow. Guides will be at HOOGE
        CRATER at 4 p.m (Two per H.Q. and four per Company)
        ROUTE. HOOGE- HELLES TRACK- JABBER TRACK.

2.   DRESS.   Haversack on back.
                 Waterproof Sheet on Waistbelt at back.
                 Rations and 2 Sandbags in haversack.
                 170 Rounds S.A.A. per man.

3.   Companies will relieve Companies as follows.-
        Right "C" relieves "B" march off at 2.30.p.m
        Left "B"   "   "D"   "   " " 2.35.p.m
        Counter-attacking Company "A" relieve "C" march off at
                                                  2.40.p.m
        Reserve Company "D" relieve "A" march off 2.45.p.m
        H.Q. will move at 2.25.p.m.

4.   All Maps, aeroplane photos etc will be taken over on
 relief.

5.   One hundred yards distance between Platoons and two
        hundred yards between Companies will be kept.

6.   Completion of relief will be notified by the outgoing
 Unit.
        For all further details see Administrative Orders No 1.
 of today.

 Issued by Orderly at
    7.30 P.M

        No1   Copy   62nd Inf Bde.
         2   "   3/4 Queens (RWS) Regt
         3   "   C.O.
         4   "   File
         5   "   "A" Coy
         6   "   "B" "
         7   "   "C" "
         8   "   "D" "
         9   "   T.O.
        10.   "   A/C.
        11   "   A/R.S.
        12   "   A/CSM. H.Q.

                            ...G.White...
                                           Captain.
                        Adjutant 19/13th Northumberland Fusiliers.

To accompany Operation Orders No 15   SECRET

12/13th NORTHUMBERLAND FUSILIERS

ADMINISTRATION ORDER No 1.

1. **RETURNS**

    As far as is known the following Returns will be required from Companies:-

RETURN	Due at Bn H.Q.	Due at Bde H.Q.
(1) Intelligence Summary for 24 hours ending 6 p.m	6.30 p.m	9.p.m
(2) Situation and Wind Report	3.30.a.m	4.a.m
(3) ditto	3.30.p.m	4 p.m
(4) Disposition Return	3 hours after taking over	5 hours after taking over
(5) Work done during the Tour in Trenches (Copy to incoming Bn)	9 a.m on day relieved	12 Noon on day of Relief.
(6) Work done up to 29th	9 a.m on 29th	12 Noon 29th
(7) Casualty Report for 24 hours ending 12 Noon	12.30 p.m	3.p.m

2. **BOMBS etc**

    All Bombs, S.O.S. Signals (1 Bomb per man and six Rifle Grenades per Rifle Grenadier) will be handed over on Relief.
    Hot Boxes and anything which may assist Cooking will be handed over on Relief. Petrol Tins will be brought out and NOT handed over.

3. **S.A.A.**

    170 Rounds of S.A.A. will be carried by all Ranks armed with Rifles, the additional 50 Rounds will be carried in the Mens pockets.

4. **PACKS**

    Packs containing Great-coats and all articles NOT to be taken to Trenches will be securely fastened, marked on the underside with Regimental No. Rank and Name, and Coy, and stacked with Orderly Room Boxes and Cooking Utensils at the Battalion Dump where the Light Railway crosses the Road at I.21.a.3.0.
    L.Cpl HOLLOWS will be in charge, Transport will collect at 4.30 p.m

5. **RATIONS**

    Rations for 27th and 28th and the Iron Ration will be carried on the Man. Waterbottles will be filled. Oil Bottles and emergency oil-can will be filled. Companies will have Tea before moving off.

6. **LOCATIONS.**

    Transport............... I.26.a.
    No 2 Coy Train........ G.35.d.7.5.
    Main Divl Grenade Store I.12.a.9.6.
    D.A.D.O.S............. H.30.c.6.5.
    Divl P of W Cage.. I.24.c.6.2.
    Divl Baths.......... I.21.a.9.6.
    Nucleus Party......... H.34.a.5.5.
    Brigade H.Q............ HOOGE CRATER.
    Dry Sock Store......... I.15.a.9.9.

1.

2.

7. **DETAILS**

Details not going into Trenches and Personnel for Courses up to November 2nd will parade at H.Q. at 3.30.p.m tomorrow to proceed to the Transport Lines.

8. **SOCKS**

A new pair of Socks for each man going to Trenches has been issued to Companies this day, each man will be in possession of three pairs of socks. One pair of dirty Socks per man will be returned to the A/Q.M. on relief for return to the Dry Sock Store.

9. **SANDBAGS**

Two Sandbags per man will be drawn by the A/Q.M. and issued to Companies with Rations.

10. **REGIMENTAL AID POST.**

The Regimental Aid Post is at J.10.a.3.3. Wounded go to MOUND thence to the Aid Post.

11. **TOOLS.**

There is a supply of Shovels in the Sub-sector. These will be taken over.

25.10.17

.... Captain.
Adjutant 12/13th Northumberland Fusiliers

WAR DIARY
or
INTELLIGENCE SUMMARY

Army Form C. 2118.

Place	Date	Hour	Summary of Events and Information	Remarks and references to Appendices
ZILLEBEKE.	Nov 1st		The 12/13 Battn. Northumberland Fusiliers marched from ZILLEBEKE BUND to "A" Camp, immediately SOUTH EAST of CHATEAU SEGARD; weather dull and inclined to rain. A Camp found to be poor as compared to other hut & tent camps in the area. Brigadier General EATER D.S.O assumed command of the 62nd Infantry Bde. Lt. Col. D.W. JOHNSON and 3.O.R joined the Battalion from 31st I.B.D.	¼ Sheet 28 Edition 3. 1/40,000
	2-4.		The Battalion remained in Reserve at "A" Camp, the period was devoted entirely to resting the men.	
	5.		The Battalion moved up into Bde Support, relieving the 8th Battn LEICESTERSHIRE REGT; the 62nd Bde taking over the Right Sector of the Division front from the 110th Inf Bde. The Battalion was disposed as follows after completion of the relief. B Coy in support the QUEENS ROYAL WEST SURREY REGT in MEBUA at J.10.A.7.8. C Coy in support to 10th Battn YORKSHIRE REGT at the BUTTE DE POLYGONE J.10.D.8.6. A and D Coys in the tunnel at CLAPHAM JUNCTION, Battn Hdqrs CLAPHAM JUNCTION. The Battn remained in Bde Support; the MEBUA occupied by B Coy was intermittently shelled after every and 2.O.R killed and 3 wounded.	BECELAERE 1/10,000
CLAPHAM JUNCTION.	6-7.			
BECELAERE.	8.		The Battalion relieved the 3/4 Battn QUEEN'S ROYAL WEST SURREY REGT in the Right sector of the Bde front; the relief was completed without casualties by 10 p.m.; after completion of relief the position was as follows. C Coy on the right holding a line of posts from J.11.C.1.4 to J.11.C.7.3. maintaining touch on the right by means of patrols with the left of the 5th Division (14th ROYAL WARWICKS) at J.10.D.70.05. B Coy on the left from holding a line of posts from J.11.E.7.3 to J.11.D.15.40; on the left B Coy had front difficulty in getting into touch with the Right part of the 1st Battn LINCOLNSHIRE REGT, which was at J.11.D.6.6. this was effected before dawn, but not without real difficulty. it was decided to dig intermediate posts forthwith.	

WAR DIARY
or
INTELLIGENCE SUMMARY

Army Form C. 2118.

Place	Date	Hour	Summary of Events and Information	Remarks and references to Appendices
REUTEL	Nov 8.		D Coy were in close support at _, one platoon at J.11.C.2.5 and one platoon at J.11.C.B.5. A Coy relieved B Coy in the MEBUS at J.10.D.8.6 (the 12/15 Batt. North'd Fusiliers took much sharper than the 3/4 Batt. QUEEN'S; the Batt. found its own support Coy). Batt. Hdqrs were at the BUTTE DE POLYGONE (J.10.A.7.8). Signal station connecting the BUTTE and Bn Hdqrs. & summer relay hut was established in MEBU at J.10.C central.	BECELAERE 1 10,000
	Nov 9.		The weather fine and day; The enemy shelled A Coy heavily between 6 and 7 AM, one man being killed & 1 wounded. A few gas shells fell in the vicinity of C Coy. On the whole a quiet day. At night prism contact was established with the 1st LINCOLNSHIRE. The establishment of a post at J.11.D.3.5 owing to heavy hostile on the PASCHENDAELE RIDGE. There was a good deal of shelling all along the front opposite BECELAERE and POLDERHOEK. Intro casualties were sustained. Many rain.	
	Nov 10.		Constant patrols at night failed to locate any enemy within 400 yards of C Coy, opposite the junction of B Coy and the 1st LINCOLNSHIRE REGT. The enemy were located in the cemetery at J.11.D.5.4; and the A Coy of this sector made communication by day with the extreme left post dangerous. Artillery quieter.	
	Nov 11.		A quiet day. 2Lt ADAMS was wounded by a sniper whilst visiting the left post of B Coy. The 1st Batt. BEDFORDSHIRE REGT relieved the 12/13 Northumberland Fusiliers in the front line, the relief having to the 15th Bde of the 5th Division at midnight. The relief was tedious & difficult owing to the rain and darkness; on relief the Northumberland Fusiliers marched to RAILWAY DUGOUTS ZILLEBEKE without casualties; Reutel was conducted via CAMERON HOUSE & JERK track.	

WAR DIARY
or
INTELLIGENCE SUMMARY
(Erase heading not required.)

Army Form C. 2118.

Instructions regarding War Diaries and Intelligence Summaries are contained in F. S. Regs., Part II. and the Staff Manual respectively. Title Pages will be prepared in manuscript.

Place	Date 1917	Hour	Summary of Events and Information	Remarks and references to Appendices
ZILLEBEKE	Nov 13		The Battalion remained at ZILLEBEKE throughout the day; every little wet & mud special attention had to be paid to feet which have become very soft; both ale also in very bad repair owing to constant use of stale oil on feet & socks to prevent trench feet.	HAZEBROUCK S.A. 1/100.000
HALLEBAST.	Nov 14.		Battn relieved at 2.30 p.m. by 3rd Battn NEW ZEALAND Rifle Bde in relief the Northumberland Fusiliers marched to MICMAC Camp, HALLEBAST. (5½ miles). Nucleus party rejoined the Battn at MICMAC.	
"	Nov 15		Battn marched from MICMAC camp to ARRAGON camp WESTOUTRE (6 miles); Battn arrived at ARRAGON camp at 1 p.m.; roads much congested owing to relief of IX th Corps by A.N.Z.A.C. Corps.	
WESTOUTRE	Nov 16.		Battn rested at ARRAGON CAMP WESTOUTRE; weather fine. 2Lt E F FRIPP arrived as a reinforcement from 31st I.B.D.	
"	Nov 17.		Battn marched from WESTOUTRE to VIEUX BERQUIN area via LOCRE and BAILLEUL; the march was done in full packs – a distance of 11 miles – without any men falling out. Weather fine; Batts well billetted in = farms over rather a wide area.	
VIEUX BERQUIN	Nov 18		Battn marched from VIEUX BERQUIN to ANNEZIN via MERVILLE and MINGES; dinners were eaten en route; packs were carried on lorries; distance marched 17 miles. Billets at ANNEZIN very good, weather fine; roads excellent.	
ANNEZIN.	Nov 19.		Battn marched from ANNEZIN via BETHUNE to HIRSIN, and went into huts in the COUPIGNY CAMP. Weather fine, roads very good, distance 9 miles.	LENS. 11 1/100.000

WAR DIARY
or
INTELLIGENCE SUMMARY

(Erase heading not required.)

Army Form C. 2118.

Instructions regarding War Diaries and Intelligence Summaries are contained in F. S. Regs, Part II. and the Staff Manual respectively. Title Pages will be prepared in manuscript.

Place	Date 19(17)	Hour	Summary of Events and Information	Remarks and references to Appendices
HERSIN	Nov 20		Weather misty & cold, Battn marched from HERSIN to MONT ST ELOI and went into FRASER CAMP, distance 8 miles. Total distance marched from ZILLEBEKE 58 miles, no men fell out. (Time taken 6 days)	LENS 11 / 100,000
MONT ST ELOI	Nov 21.		Heavy rain, Battn marched from MONT ST ELOI to MAROEUIL and went into rest billets in the XIIIth Corps area; No Battn. drill billeted in the COTTON FACTORY.	
MAROEUIL	Nov 22		62nd Bde relieved a Bde of the 47th Division as part of the Reserve Division of the XIII" Corps. Bde HQrs established at ECURIE.	
"	Nov 23.		Lt Col EDLMANN and Coy Commanders reconnoitred the GAVRELLE trenches, now held by 31st Division with a view to a possible advancement of the enemy consequent upon the advance of the IIIrd army in front of CAMBRAI. (in which case the XXIst Division is to pass through the XXIst Div & pursue the enemy.)	
"	Nov 24		Lt & Qualtermaster G.C. JACKSON, Lt A.M. SEMPLE and 2 Lt DAVIES returned for duty from 31st I.B.D. also reinforcement of 6.O.R.	
"	Nov 25.		Battn resting at MAROEUIL, LIEUT J.R. RITZEMA reported for duty from 31st I.B.D.	
"	Nov 26 -29		Training in musketry and bayonet fighting carried out ; persistent rumours of the move of the 21st Division from the Western to some other Allied front are heard on all sides; it is decided by the Brigadier General Commanding that training should be regulated with a view to proceeding to the Italian front. Small drafts arrived from 1st Garrison Battn. Northumberland Fusiliers (now at Malta)	

Army Form C. 2118.

WAR DIARY
or
INTELLIGENCE SUMMARY
(Erase heading not required.)

Instructions regarding War Diaries and Intelligence Summaries are contained in F. S. Regs., Part II. and the Staff Manual respectively. Title Pages will be prepared in manuscript.

Place	Date	Hour	Summary of Events and Information	Remarks and references to Appendices
MAROEUIL	Nov 29		The draft numbered 58 O.R. in all; & are confirmed of men physically unfit in 1914 but are well up to the physical standard. All officers & men on courses recalled, leave to England cancelled.	LENS 11 / 100.000
	Nov 30		Orders received to be ready move to 'a new area'; training continued. J Millman Lt Col Commanding 12/13 Batln Northumberland Fusiliers Nov 30th 1917	

WAR DIARY or INTELLIGENCE SUMMARY

Army Form C. 2118.

12/13 R. North. Fusiliers Dec 1917

Place	Date	Hour	Summary of Events and Information	Remarks and references to Appendices
PERONNE	1st	7.30am	The Battalion awoke from MAROEUIL and detrained at 4.30am. Marched to CARTIGNY when Billets consisting of NISSEN huts and Cellars of battered Buildings was made. Hd Qrs, 3rd Bn, 3rd Division came under the orders of VII Corps on arrival. Strength of Battalion 41 Officers and 684 OR. HQ and 31 TBD the Battalion left CARTIGNY and moved into Camp at LONGAVESNES, the	
LONGAVESNES	2nd	1.30pm	Division took over the BEPAUME Sector, 62 Inf Bde being in Divisional Reserve.	
	3rd		Route Marching to various areas was resumed by all officers of the Battalion. the Battalion "stood to" each morning and Training was carried out each day.	
	4th			
	5th		Second Lieuts G.C.W. PRINGLE and C. BUGLISS departed for duty from 16 North Irish.	
	6th		Lieut Colonel E.S. CHANCE 2nd Dragoon Guards (Queen Bays) assumed command of the Battalion and Lieut Colonel F.J.F. EDMANN, DSO left for England.	
	7th			
	8th		Second Lieuts A. WILLIAMSON and W.L.C. HUTTON reported for duty from 16 North Irish.	
PEZIERE	9th		62 Inf Bde returned back to the line on the departure of the Divisional front, thus Battalion were relieved in Brigade reserve. Relief completed by 5pm. A.B and C Coys and Batt HQ on Railway Embankment in W.23.b, about 1000 yards North West of PEZIERE and D Coy in "BROWN LINE" in W.18.a b and d.	
	10th		5 coy relieve W.L.C. HUTTON were admitted to hospital sick	

Reference Map Sheet 57/C SE H 1/20,000

WAR DIARY
or
INTELLIGENCE SUMMARY.

(Erase heading not required.)

Army Form C. 2118.

Oct Continued

Place	Date	Hour	Summary of Events and Information	Remarks and references to Appendices
PÉZIÈRE	10th	9 pm	On receipt of orders from 62 Inf Bde to move B Company into CAVALRY LINE Company was moved forward and occupied CAVALRY LINE in W 18 b and	
	11th		X 13 a.	
	12th		24 O.R. arrived from 31 I.B.D. Lieut Q master G.C. TURNER was admitted to hospital sick.	
	13th		2nd Lieut V.C. CHERRYMAN was admitted to hospital with an injured knee caused by a fall from a horse. For dispositions see Sketch map (Appx 30.1 + No 2.) Battn was forced with or Railway Embankment during the tour of duty in Caverns.	Appx 1.- Appx 2.1
	13 Bd	11:30	The Battalion relieved 10 YORK.R in the right sub sector of the Left Brigade Sector. The relief was completed by 6.30 p.m, marched by night was heavy 19 OR arrived from 31 I.B.D. Front and Support were our water down. Grass and trails were reconnoitred Enemy activity was normal	Appx 3.-
	14th			
	15th		Hostile artillery were active, the ridge at X 25 a and our front line at X 19 c were somewhat heavily shelled. Second Lieut G. JACKSON was wounded and admitted to hospital, 3 OR were killed and 3 OR wounded. Patrolling was active and little was seen of the enemy	

WAR DIARY
or
INTELLIGENCE SUMMARY.
(Erase heading not required.)

Army Form C. 2118.

Place	Date	Hour	Summary of Events and Information	Remarks and references to Appendices
PEZIÈRE	16d	—	Second Lieut. D. SKIPSEY reported from 31 I.B.D. Army Artillery activity was normal. A patrol under Captain D.E.F. WRIGHT consisting of Lieut. G. NOBLE and 8 O.R. succeeded in locating a source of advanced fire at X.14.c.60.55	Appx 4, Appx 5
	17d		Enemy activity normal. The Barracks were relieved by 15 D.L.I. the relief was completed by 6.30 pm.	Appx 6
			Appendices "A" and "B" show dispositions and Orders taken respectively. A wiring party of work out. Attached hereto in a report of movements from 13/8 November to 18 Sept. Bn move to Divisional reserve by 4 on relief by 62 Sgt Bn. Occupied huts at HEUDICOURT — Organization ordered in Appx no 4	Appx 4
HEUDICOURT.	Nd.		Officers reconnaissances were carried in 62 St Bn Defence Scheme "A and B" (Appx 8)	Appx 8
	19d		Working parties were turned for wiring Railway Embankment Company Parades and Brigade training was continued with Dear with measure	
	24d 25d		Officers reconnoitring the left sub sector of the Divisional front. Church Bay Bn Runner company of packing etc. was forward for the move, and a Battalion Concert was during the evening.	

WAR DIARY
or
INTELLIGENCE SUMMARY

Army Form C. 2118.

Place	Date	Hour	Summary of Events and Information	Remarks and references to Appendices
HEUDICOURT	1917 Dec. 26th	—	Lieut H.F. GREENE left the Battalion	
		7pm	The Battalion relieved 1 E.YORK.R in the left Sub Sector being completed by 8.30pm. The Battalion was disposed as follows:— Right: D. Coy and H.Q. at X.12.b.25.30 Right: B " HQ at Y.C.15.30 Left: A " HQ at X.13.a.15.18 Support: C " HQ at X.13.a.15.65 Reserve: Battalion H.Q. at X.13.a.2.5. The 9th Seaforth Rifles (on the right of the 9th Division) were on the left of the Battalion and the 3/4 Queens (R.W.S.R.) on the right.	Appx 9
	27/12		Slow methodical hostile activity. Enemy snipers were active by day and by night as far as the moonlight permitted. Patrolling was carried out by night.	
	28/12			
	29/12		Wiring was carried out by 14 parties. Two (?) on the nights 28/29 and 29/30. 186 coils of wire were put out and the whole front strengthened. The right & left of the right Company area has been connected by means of a communication trench and the right Company area linked made continuous. A communication trench is being dug from the railway (near left Coy H.Q.) etc	

WAR DIARY
INTELLIGENCE SUMMARY

Army Form C. 2118.

Place	Date	Hour	Summary of Events and Information	Remarks and references to Appendices
	1914 Dec			
	30d		Dec 1914 Continued	
			to the left of the front line, a ricketic the sector held by the left Company has been inaccessible by day halcons etc having to be taken up after dusk.	
			A draft of 4 Q.O.R. joined the Battalion from 3rd I.B.D.	
			Major A.E. SCOTT and Lieut. A.P. HARROWER reported for duty.	
			The following relief took place on the night 30/31st.	
			"D" Coy on the right was relieved by "C" Company	
			"B" Coy on the left was relieved by "A" Company	Appx 9
			Sketch map showing dispositions after relief is attached as Appendix 9. W.O.= Appx 11.	Appx 11
	31st		having unusual happened during the night 30/31st, a thorough examination of disused gun-pits and dug-outs in wood running from X.2.0.4 to X.13.b.9 & H. by a force under Lieut R.H. COMBET. At 10.15 a.m. 1916 the enemy shelled for about ten minutes from 10.55 to 11.5 – Lewisey time 11.55 – 12.5 am, some of the shells few tear ou trenches but as thought that back areas were shelled.	
			STRENGTH	
			Effective 40 Officers	MHS Ordu under
			Lionel 811 Officers	H/S — do —

R. Hawer Lieut Colonel
Comdg 17/3rd B. Border R.

12/13th Northumberland Fusiliers.

DEFENCE SCHEME ETC.

APPENDIX No 1.

1. DISPOSITION.

   ONE Coy in "Cavalry Line" which is held as follows by tonight:
   (a) Advanced Lewis gun Post about W.18.b.9.4.
   (b) Platoon Post about W.18.b.9.3.
   (c) Platoon Post about W.18.b.6.3.
   Coy H.Q. at W.18.b.9.2.

   BY DAY the Coy is withdrawn to shelters in Sunken Road from W.18.b.9.0 to W.18.b.8.3 with Coy H.Q. at X.13.c.3.5.

   The "Cavalry Line" is in view of the enemy. Men should not be allowed to walk about near it by day.

   ONE Coy in "Brown Line" between W.18.a.75.40 and W.18.d.8.4.
   Coy H.Q. at W.18.a.9.3.
   This line is held by two strong posts.

   Two Coys and Battn H.Q. are situated on S. side of Railway Embankment in W.23.b.

2. ACTION IN CASE OF ATTACK.
   Both the "Cavalry Line" and the "Brown Line" will be held at all costs.
   Battn H.Q. and the 2 Coys in the railway Embankment will be held in readiness to be used as a Bde reserve.

3. VICKERS GUNS are situated as shewn on attached map.

4. COMMUNICATION. The Coys in the Cavalry and Brown Line are both in telephonic communication with Battn H.Q.
   There is telephone and visual signalling communication from Battn. to Bde H.Q.

5. S.A.A. The Coy in the "Cavalry Line" has 4 S.A.A. boxes in reserve at their H.Q.
   The Coy in the "Brown Line" has 6 S.A.A. boxes in reserve at their H.Q.
   There is a S.A.A. and Grenade Dump at Battn H.Q.

6. R.E. MATERIAL is drawn from the dump at W.18.d.8.1.

7. COOKING. Battn H.Q. and the 2 Coys in the railway embankment use the Cookers which are close to Battn H.Q.
   There is a Cookhouse at about W.18.b.10.05 which is used by the two forward Coys. About 40 petrol tins are now here.
   A watercart is kept at Battn H.Q.

8. OBSERVATION POST. The Battn finds a Bde Observation post in the "Cavalry Line". This post will be in telephonic communication with Bde H.Q.

WORK REQUIRED TO BE CARRIED OUT.

(a) CAVALRY LINE.   Improvement of the Trenches occupied by by the platoon posts and the advanced Lewis Gun posts.
More duckboards are required and more wire on front of the trench.

(b) BROWN LINE. Improvement of the platoon posts. More duckboards required. Improvement of shelters which are at present in the fire trench, but should be in saps.

(c) BURIAL OF HORSES.   There are 3 or 4 more which should be buried.

13.12.17.

(Signed) E S. CHANCE.
................Lt.Col.
Commanding B E A R.

APPENDIX No 2.

From SHEET 57C S.E.4.

SCALE = 1/10000

13

CAVALRY LINE

1 Company

BROWN LINE

1 Company.

18

W X

24

Garsin Wall
Copse

2 Companies
and
Bn H.Q.

17

23

12/13th NORTHUMBERLAND FUSILIERS
OPERATION ORDER No. 36

SECRET
Copy No. 3
12.12.17

Ref. Sheet
57c.S.E.

1. **RELIEF.** The Battalion will relieve the 10th Battn Yorks Regt in the Right Sub-Sector of the Brigade Front on the evening of the 13th inst. as follows:-
   "C" Coy 12/13th North'd Fus will relieve "A" Coy 10th Yorks. Regt on the RIGHT.
   "A" Coy 12/13th North'd Fus will relieve "B" Coy 10th Yorks Regt in the CENTRE
   "B" Coy 12/13th North'd Fus will relieve "D" Coy 10th Yorks Regt on the LEFT.
   "D" Coy 12/13th North'd Fus will relieve "C" Coy 10th Yorks Regt in RESERVE.
   Battn. Headquarters will be in House at W.30.c.95.80
   DRESS:- ASSAULTING ORDER. Leather Jerkins will be worn.
   Companies move off at 4.30 p.m

2. **GUIDES.** Guides, three per Coy from 10th Yorks Regt will meet Companies as follows:-
   For "A" Coy at "B" Coy H.Q. of 10th Yorks Regt
   For "C" "   " "A" "   "   "   "   "   "
   For "B" "   " Cross Rds W.18.d.8.1 from 4.30 p.m
   For "D" "   "   ditto   "   ditto

3. **ADVANCED PARTIES** Advanced parties of 1 Officer, 1 N.C.O. and 1 Runner per Company will report for Guides at Battn H.Q. 10th Yorks Regt at 10 a.m. to proceed to take over Stores etc in Company areas.

4. **STORES.** All Grenades, S.A.A., S.O.S. Signals, Defence Schemes etc will be taken over.
   Companies will also hand over all Trench Stores etc in their present areas to relieving Coys of 10th Yorks Regt. Lists of Stores handed over and taken over will be forwarded to Battn H.Q. by 9 a.m 14th inst.

5. **COMPLETION of RELIEF.** Completion of Relief will be notified to Battn H.Q. by the Code word "JACK"

6. **RELIEVING UNIT.** 10th Yorks Regt will take over positions in Brigade Reserve vacated by Companies.
   Advanced parties from Coys of 10th Yorks Regt taking over will report at Coys H.Q. in the afternoon of 13th inst. Guides will be found by "B" and "D" Coys as follows:-
   3 from "B" Coy for "D" Coy 10th Yorks Regt
   3 "   "D" "   " "C" "   "   "   "
   Guides will be at Cross Roads W. 18.d.8.1 at 5.15.p.m

7. Further ADMINISTRATION ORDERS are being issued separately.

ISSUED BY ORDERLY AT
3.30 p.m
    Copy No 1   62nd Inf. Bde.
          2   C. O.
          3   File
          4   "A" Coy
          5   "B" "
          6   "C" "
          7   "D" "
          8   Q.M.
          9   R.S.M.
         10   T.O.
         11   10th Yorks Regt.

J McKinnon
Captain

SECRET

ADMINISTRATIVE ORDERS.

Teas will be at 3.30 p.m. tomorrow.
Men will wear Leather jerkins; washing and shaving kit
   in the haversack.
Waterbottles will be filled.
Packs containing Great coats and marked will be stacked
      by Coys as follows:-
            A & C Coys at Coy H.Q. under guard
            B & D Coys will stack packs in the afternoon
                at Bde R.E. Dump under guard.
   Packs will be collected from these dumps by returning
ration wagons.

COOKING.   Cooking on the cookers for C, D and H.Q. Coys
will be done in the SUNKEN ROAD near Battn H.Q.
1 Watercart will be at this point at 5 p.m.
Rations for the above Coys will be dumped at this point.
Cooking for A & B Coys will be done in Cookhouse in the
new area of the Support Platoon of B Coy along Railway
Embankment.
Rations for A & B Coys will be dumped at the ration Dump
at X.13.c.3.1 at 5.30 p.m.
Coys will arrange for 1 N.C.O. and 1 man per Company to
be left in charge of their rations at the above Dumps until
collected.

40 petrol tins will be handed over to 10th YORK R. at the
present Cookhouse of D & C Coys; and 40 petrol tins will
be taken over by A & B Coys in their new Cookhouse.
40 petrol tins will be taken over at Battn H.Q.
The T.O. 12/13th Northumberland Fus) will arrange to
hand over 40 petrol tins to T.O. 10th YORK R.
Arrangements are being made to increase supply of petrol
tins at new Cookhouse of A & B Coys.

R.E. DUMPS.   The LEFT Coy draw R.E. Material at W.18.d.8.1.
              Limbers will take R.E. Material for other
Coys to about X.19.c.5.4.

............................Captain
   Adjutant B E A R

   Copy No. 1 62nd Inf Bde.
            2 C.O.
            3 File
            4 A Coy
            5 B
            6 C
            7 D
            8 Q.M.
            9 T.O.
           10 R.S.M.

Appendix No 3

RIGHT SUB SECTOR. LEFT BRIGADE.

DEFENCE SCHEME.

"BEAR"

Ref. Sheet 57c.S E 4
and sketch map attached.

1. DISPOSITIONS.

The front line is held by two Companies,

(a) RIGHT COY.
No.1.Post. Not held by day, but held by night by 1.L.G.Section & 1.Rifle Section, (about 18.O.R.).

No.2.Post. Held by one platoon and 1.extra L.G.Section (3.L.Guns in all).

Support. 1 Rifle Section.

(b) LEFT COY.
No.1 Post. 1.Platoon (2.Lewis Guns).

No.2.Post. 1.Platoon (2. Lewis Guns).

SUPPORT COY.
By day in huts and dug outs on Railway.
By night in BROWN LINE.
No.1.Post.   1.Platoon.
No.2.Post.   1.Platoon.

RESERVE COY.   As shewn on sketch.
If accomodation could be made for the RESERVE Coy further back, either on the railway at W94d or 200/300 yds. in rear of its present position, the Support Coy might have one platoon where it is at present, and one platoon where the RESERVE Coy is now.
Until good accomodation can be provided for the RESERVE Coy in one of the places suggested it is considered better to keep the SUPPORT and RESERVE Coys in their present positions.

BATTALION H.QRS.   House at W.30.C.85.80.

2. DEFENCE.

(a). The front line is the main line of resistance and will be held to the last.
In case of alarm the whole Battalion will "stand to"

(b) Should the enemy gain a footing in the front line the Company concerned will immediately eject him.

P.T.O.

Appx 4

OPERATION ORDER NO. 36   SECRET
                         Copy No. 3

Ref Sh. 57c S.E.

1. RELIEF.   The Battn will be relieved by the
              15th D.L.I. in the Right sub-sector of
              the Bde Front on the evening of the
              17th inst as follows:-
              "A" Coy 12/13th N.F. on the LEFT will be
                     relieved by "D" Coy 15th D.L.I.
              "B" Coy 12/13th N.F. in SUPPORT will be
                     relieved by "B" Coy 15th D.L.I.
              "C" Coy 12/13th on the RIGHT will be
                     relieved by "A" Coy 15th D.L.I.
              "D" Coy 12/13th N.F. in RESERVE will be
                     relieved by "C" Coy 15th D.L.I.
              On completion of relief the Battn will
              occupy MIDDLESEX CAMP, NEUDECOURT to which
              companies will march independently.

2. ADVANCE PARTY.   Coys will detail 1 N.C.O. and
              3 men to report at Battn H.Q. by 6 a.m.
              17th with the unexpended portion of their
              rations, to take over Camp to be occupied
              by the Battn.   The Officer in charge
              of the party will arrange for a guide
              for each Coy to be at X Rds RAILTON by
              5.30 p.m. to meet the Coys.

3. RELIEVING UNIT.   Advance parties from Coys of
              15th D.L.I. will report to Coy H.Qs. by
              2.30 p.m. on the 17th inst.   Party for
              Battn H.Q. at 2 p.m.
              Guides will be arranged for Coys concerned.

                         - 1 -

- 2 -

4. STORES. Coys will hand over all grenades, Rifle grenades, S.A.A, S.O.S. Signals, Tools, Defence Schemes and maps showing the defences. Lists of stores &c. handed over will be forwarded to Battn H.Q. by 10 a.m. on the 18th inst.

5. COMPLETION OF RELIEF. Completion of relief will be notified to Battn H.Q. by code word "MARRY" before moving off. Coy Commanders will report personally to Commanding Officer on arrival in Camp.

ADMINISTRATIVE ORDERS will be issued later to those concerned.

G.W.Lacey
.... 2nd Lieut for
Adjt. B E A R. Captain

16.12.17

Copy No. 1 Bde
         2 C.O.
         3 File
         4 A Coy
         5 B
         6 C
         7 D
         8 T.O.
         9 Q.M.
        10 15 D.L.I.
        11 R.S.M.

Acknowledge

The Right Coy will employ for this purpose the section in support in the BROWN LINE about x 19a.3.0. Attack will be made across across the open.

The LEFT Company having both platoons in the Front line will employ platoon or sections inaffected.

(c) The SUPPORT Coy. will hold the BROWN LINE.

(d) The RESERVE Coy will be prepared to counter attack on instructions from Bn.Hd Qrs. If the situation demands immediate action Company Commander will act on his own initiative, reporting action taken to Bn.H.Q. phone

(e). Officers & Section Commanders of the SUPPORT & RESERVE Coys must know all the way forward to the front line, and mark the openings in the wire conspicuously with white tape, paper or tins.

(f) Coy Commanders will keep Bn.H.Q. constantly informed of the situation.

3. S.A.A.GRENADES etc. Dumps are at Batt and Coy.H.Qrs.

4. S.O.S.SIGNAL. When the S.O.S.Signal is put up all Batteries on the Divisional front will open fire for five minutes and then stop unless the signal is repeated, and unless it is clear that a serious attack is in progress.

If the S.O.S.Signal is sent up between 6.a.m. and 8.a.m. fire will be kept up for 15.minutes without further instructions.

S.O.S.Signal now in use is 2.Green and 2.White lights fired by means of a Rifle Grenade.

DECEMBER 16th.1917.

Lieut.Col.
O.C. B E A R.

Dear Sefton
Ashburn

Appx 6.

RIGHT SUB-SECTOR (BEAR)

LEFT BRIGADE.

WORK COMPLETED
and in PROGRESS - 6 h.m DEC. 16/17

R/- Stahl wahr
abantir.

FRONT LINE

1. WIRE. RIGHT COY. Wiring in front of No 1
and No 2 Posts is completed.
This is in good condition and
thick.

LEFT COY. The whole of the company
front is wired but requires
thickening in places. This
work is in progress.

2. PLATOON POSTS. Posts Nos. 1 and 2 are nearly
completed. Trench 6 feet wide
at top, with fire bays built
for elbow. Further work required.
Posts Nos 3 and 4 have been
dug sufficiently deep and wide
and fire steps constructed.
Berms to parapet and
parados are being made.

3. COMMUNICATION
TRENCH. A communication trench has
been dug from No 1 Post trench
to about 80 yards from the

BROWN LINE. This allows the
front line to be approached under
cover from observation. Further work
on this trench will be required.

4. SHELTERS   RIGHT COY. Three shelters
each for 2 or 3 men have been
completed. Two shelters each
for 16 to 20 men are under
construction.

LEFT COY. One shelter has been
completed and two others
are still under construction.
Accommodation for about 40 men
in all.

5. LATRINES   Latrines have been made for
each post. Further improvements
required.

SUPPORT COY
about 150 yards of the BROWN
LINE in X.19.a. has been
deepened and repaired.
The trench is now in good order,
with fire step.

RESERVE COY
about 200 yards of the
BROWN LINE in X.19.c. have been
deepened and repaired. Moderate
shelter for about 80 men, and
3 latrines have been constructed

3

and some trench boards put
down.
Owing to numerous trench boards not
being available, there are as yet very
few in the front line.

P. Maxwell / Lt Col.
OZ BEAR

Dec. 16/17
D. 8-fr. 2n/

Appendix No. 6

APPENDIX N° 5.
From SHEET 57c. SE
Scale = 1/10000.

LEFT COY
RIGHT COY
RIGHT COY
SUPPORT COY
RES. COY
PEIZIERE

SECRET

ADMINISTRATIVE ORDERS.

1. ADVANCE PARTY.   2/Lt. J.W.ELLIOTT will be in
    charge of Advance party detailed in O.O.36

2. TRANSPORT. The Battn Transport and Q.M.
    stores will move to the new Camp tomorrow
    17th inst.
        Transport Officer will arrange for
    one Limber Wagon and the Mess Cart to
    report at Battn H.Q. at 3 p.m. tomorrow.

3. TRANSPORT DETAILS. Transport Officer will
    arrange for all details at present with
    the Transport to proceed to the New Camp
    by 11 a.m. tomorrow; they will report to
    2nd-Lt. J.W.ELLIOTT.

4. COOKERS. Transport Officer will arrange for
    horses to take the cookers to the new Camp
    to report at 1.30 p.m.   A guide will meet
    the Cookers at X-Roads RAILTON at 2.30 p.m.
    Tea will be served when the Coys arrive in
    Camp.

5. SOCKS. Q.M. will arrange for dry socks to be
    at new camp for Coys to change on arrival.

6. PETROL TINS. "B" Coy will arrange for 30
    petrol tins from their cookhouse to be
    returned to Bn H.Q. by 2 p.m. tomorrow.

7. RATIONS. On and from the 18th inst. and until
    further notice rations will be delivered
    by No. 2 Coy, 21st Div. Train, to LONGAVESNES
    CHURCH at 8 a.m. each morning.   T.O. will
    arrange to draw same.

- 1 -

- 2 -

5. WATER SUPPLY. Waterpoints are situated at:-
   ST.EMILE, SAULCOURT, EPEHY.

6. FUEL. Div. Fuel Dump in Buire closes at
   2 p.m. 16th and opens at same hour at
   LONGAVESNES on the 17th.

G.W.Lacey.
.................2nd Lieut.
for Adjt B E A R-

16.12.17

Appendix
No.4

Apps 8

DEFENCE SCHEME
12/13th Northumberland Fusiliers

Dec. 17/1917.   Ref:- Maps
                          57C.S.E 1/20000
                          62C.N.E 1/20000

1. Alternative Courses of Action

   The 62nd Inf. Bde. will be prepared to

   i. Deliver a counter-attack on any part of the Divisional Front.

   ii. To hold that portion of the Corps Line, within the Divisional area; this would only be necessary if the villages of EPEHY and PEIZIERE had been taken.

   iii. To hold the ground between PEIZIERE and REVELON FARM as a support to the BROWN LINE (Scheme A.)

   iv. To form a defensive flank, pivoting on EPEHY - PEIZIERE,
        facing N.E — (Scheme B)
          "   S.E — (Scheme C)

2. Scheme A
   The General Line to be held by the Brigade will be —

2.

(a) <u>FRONT LINE</u> the Railway from
~~W.30b~~. 0.8. to W.23.a.9.1.

(b) <u>SUPPORT LINE</u> from the strong
point at W.30.c.8.7 westwards
to the spur which runs
through W.23 c and d, thence
northwards along this spur
to RAILTON (<u>inclusive</u>.)

(c) Action to be taken by the
12/13th North^d Fus^{rs}
B and D Companies will
hold the line of the Railway
  B Coy from ~~W.30.c~~ X.25.a 0.8.
        to   W.24.d.0.6.
  D Coy from W.24.d.0.6
        to   W.23.a.9.1.
A. and C Coys will be
in support along the ROAD
from W.30.b.6.3 to level
crossing at W.23.b.1.1.
  A Coy from W.30.b.6.3
        to   W.24.c.4.1
  C Coy from W.24.c.4.1 to
        level crossing at W.23.b.1.1.

(d) Bn H.Q. will be at W.30.c.9.8.

3.

SCHEME B

(a) The General line to be held by the Brigade will be the PEIZIERE – HEUDECOURT Road (through W.29a and b. and W.22.c) with the right flank resting in the Strong Point at W.30.c.8.7. A forward line of posts will be held along the Railway as in Scheme A.

(b) Action to be taken by the 12/13th Northld Fus:—

B Coy will hold the line of the Railway from W.25.a.8 to W.23.a.9.1. by a series of posts

D Coy will hold the line from
W.30.c.8.7.
to W.30.a.3.2

C. Coy from W.30.a.3.2
to W.29.b.3.4

A Coy from W.29.b.3.4
to W.29.a.3.7

C. Position of Bn H.Q will be notified later

4.

4. <u>SCHEME C.</u>

(a) The Brigade will hold the General Line from the Strong Point at 7.1.c.8.0 thence along the EPEHY – VILLERS FAUCON road

(b) Action to be taken by the 12/13th Northd Fus:rs. —
Battalion will move to a position of assembly in E9c West of SAULCOURT and SE of road running from E4c.4.0 through E9 central.

5. <u>BRIGADE Hd.Qrs. will in all cases move to E10a.1.3.</u>

6. If the Battalion is ordered to move to a "Position of readiness" in accordance with one of the above schemes the Battalion will take up a position of readiness in dead ground behind the line to be taken up.

7. Schemes A and B will be rehearsed by all officers and N.C.O's on the morning of Dec. 19

- 5 -

Further instructions will be issued later

8. The Battalion will also be prepared to move under the direct orders of the B.G.C Left Brigade (64th Inf. Bde.)

December 17/1917

Lt. Col
O.C. BEAR.

Copy No 1 O.C. "A" Coy
"   2 " B "
"   3 " C "
"   4 " D "
"   5 I.O.
"   6 L.G.O.
"   7 Commanding Officer
"   8 File

Appendix
No 8.

12/13th NORTHUMBERLAND FUSILIERS.

OPERATION ORDER NO. 58   24.12.17
Ref. Map Sh. 57 c S.E.   Copy No..... 2.
1/20,000

    RELIEF.
1. The 62nd Inf Bde. will relieve the 64th Inf. Bde. in the Left Sub-sector of the Divisional Front on 26th Dec 1917.
The Bn will relieve the 1st E. YORKSHIRE REGT. in the left sub-sector of the Bde Front on evening of 26th Dec. as follows:-

  "D" Coy 12/13th N.F. "B" Coy 1 E.Yorks.Rgt Right Front
  "B" do   "A" do   Left "
  "C" do   "C" do   RIGHT Support
  "A" do   "D" do   LEFT "

Battn H.Q. will be at X.13.a.2.5.

D Coy ORDER OF MARCH: as per margin. 1st Coy move off at 3.30 p.m.
B   100 yards interval between platoons; 300 yards interval
C   between Coys, must be maintained.
H.Q.   DRESS: Assaulting order, leather jerkins will be worn.
A
2. GUIDES 3 per Coy will meet the Coys at RAILTON Cross Rds from 3.45 p.m. on 26th inst.

3. ADVANCED PARTIES. Advanced parties of 1 Officer, 1 N.C.O. and 1 Runner per Coy will report at H.Qs. of Coys of 1st E. Yorks R. on the 26th inst as follows:
Front line Coys "B" and "D" by 6.45 a.m.
"A" and "C" Coys & H.Q. by 2 p.m.
Battn Intelligence Officer will report at H.Q. 1st E. Yorks R. at 2 p.m. on 26th.

4. TRENCH STORES.
All Grenades, S.A.A., S.O.S. Signals, Tools, Defence Schemes etc. will be taken over. Lists of stores taken over and location of Coy Trench Store dumps will be forwarded to Battn H.Q. by 9 a.m. on 27th Dec.

5. COMPLETION OF RELIEF.
Completion of relief will be notified to Battn H.Q. by code word "ARNOLD".

6. WORKING PARTY. A Working Party of 1 N.C.O. and 32 men will be found by "A" Coy each night at 5 p.m. commencing 26th inst. Party will be employed in carrying timber from wagons of 178th Tunnelling Coy. at W.18.b.5.8 to railway embankment X.13.a. Further details will be issued later.

7. ADMINISTRATIVE ORDERS. Further Administrative Orders will be issued later.

8. A C K N O W L E D G E.

                                                                ....Captain
24.12.17   Adj 12/13th Northd Fusiliers.

    Copy No. 1 62nd Inf Bde   No. 10 R.S.M.
         2 C.O.   11 1st E.Yorks R.
         3 File & War Diary
         4 A Coy
         5 B
         6 C
         7 D
         8 T.O.
         9 Q.M.

ADMINISTRATIVE INSTRUCTIONS.

1. The Transport will move today to VILLERS FAUCON, taking over lines at present occupied by 64th Inf Bde. Further instructions will be issued to the T.O.

2. Orders re Officers valises & blankets have already been issued. Officers mess boxes will be at Battn H.Q. by 2.30 p.m today. The Mess cart will be at Bn H.Q. in the line by 4.15 p.m.
The T.O. will arrange for a limber to convey officers trench kits to trenches to be at Bn H.Q. at 2.30 p.m.

   T.O. & L.G.O. will arrange for L.G. Limbers to convey L.Gs. and magazines etc. to Battn H.Q. in the line, leaving present camp by 3.15 p.m. 1 L.G., N.C.O. per Coy will accompany the limbers in charge of the guns of their Coys.
   The T.O. will arrange for transport to convey the R.E. Stores at present at Q.M. Stores to Battn H.Q. in the line tonight.
   A supply of timber and wood fuel will also be sent to Bn H.Q.

3. COOKING ARRANGEMENTS.
   Cooking for all Coys while in the line will be carried out behind the Railway embankment in X.13.a. Cookers will not be brought up but cooking will be on dixies.
   B & D Coys in front line:
      Breakfast 6.30 a.m. prompt.
      Hot tea will be taken up in Hot food containers along with Breakfast at 6 a.m. and issued at 12 noon.
      Dinners will be at 5 p.m.
      A Hot meal (tea or porridge) will be issued at 11.30 p.m.
   A & C Coys In support & H.Q.
      Breakfast 7.30 a.m.
      Dinner 12.30 p.m.
      Tea 5.30 p.m.
      Hot meal (if available) 11.30 p.m.
   WATER. Both water carts will come up each night to Battn H.Q. and fill up dixies, petrol tins, and water supply tanks. Two journeys will be necessary.
   90 petrol tins will be taken over at Bn H.Q.

4. Rations will be brought up to Battn H.Q. after dusk each night. Rations for tomorrow 27th will be brought up by Transport tonight.
   R.E. MATERIAL. A dump will be formed under Battn arrangements at Battn H.Q. The material will be brought there in limbers.

5. CARE OF FEET. Men will take 2 pairs of dry socks with them into the line in addition to the pair being worn.
   Platoon Commanders are responsible that every man in his platoon has his feet rubbed at least once a day and his socks changed daily. Men must be given as much exercise as possible to keep their feet warm. Coys will send in their wet socks to Battn H.Q. on 27th and following days and receive dry socks in return.
   Q.M. will arrange for first supply of dry socks to come up on 27th and daily afterwards.

6. SALVAGE. The necessity of salvaging rifles, S.A.A., and all other forms of equipment must be impressed on all officers and O.Rs. Each Coy will establish a salvage dump near its H.Q. & arrange to send the material daily to the Dump at Bn H.Q. Each Coy will detail 1 man and "A" Coy 1 L/Cpl in addition to form a Battn salvage party which will permanently live at Bn H.Q. The men detailed will report to O.C. H.Q. Coy at 6 p.m. on the 26th inst.

- 1 -

- 2 -

The duties of this salvage party will be to salvage all articles in the area behind Battn H.Q. to take charge of the Battn salvage dump, and to see that articles in it are sent back daily to the Transport lines on the returning ration vehicles.

..........................Captain
Adjt 12/13th Northumberland Fusiliers.

26.12.17

INSTRUCTIONS.

1. **STAND-TO.**
   Morning 6 a.m. – 7 a.m.
   Evening 3.45 p.m. – 4.45 p.m.

2. **PROGRAMME OF WORK.**
   Coys will render to Battn H.Q. by 8.30 a.m. daily commencing 26th inst a programme for the next 24 hours.
   Coys will render also to Battn H.Q. by 8.30 a.m. a report of work done during previous 24 hours.

3. **PATROLS.**
   Coys will arrange for protective patrols to cover their front from 4 a.m. – 7 a.m. daily. Officers and N.C.Os. who have no or little experience in patrol work will be sent out on patrol with experienced officers or N.C.Os.

4. **CONCEALMENT FROM VIEW.** It is impossible on a clear day to reach the Front Line except on the right without being exposed to view. No officer or man will therefore go up to the front line across the open on a clear day. Officers will prevent officers or men of other units doing this.

5. **S.O.S.ROCKETS.**
   The following will be the procedure with regard to positions of S.O.S. rockets in sector to be taken over.
   At each Coy H.Q. & Bn H.Q. 2 rifles to be kept in a rack.
   In addition to the above:
   In Front Line of "B" Coy –
       2 rifles to be kept in a rack) These racks will
   In detached post "D" Coy –   ) be at place where
       2 rifles to be kept in a rack) platoon officer
) sleeps.
   The S.O.S. Rifles will be kept loaded with blank cartridge and the Grenade rod in them. The Grenade will be kept in tin close by.
   The O.C. Coy will be responsible that the S.O.S. rifles are kept clean.
   Where there are not sufficient S.O.S. rifles taken over, on the above scale, rifles to complete should be salved.
   The Pioneers will make the necessary racks if Coys do not take over sufficient.

6. **LISTS** of Returns due from Coys are attached.

                                                ....Captain
                                          Adj 12/13th Northd Fusrs.

25.12.17

WAR DIARY or INTELLIGENCE SUMMARY

Army Form C. 2118.

12th Batt. North Fusiliers

January 1918 Vol 29

Place	Date	Hour	Summary of Events and Information	Remarks and references to Appendices
Headquarters Kemmel Huts Shed 54c S.E. Bailleul H.A.	January 10th 1918	P.M.	A quiet day, nothing unusual occurred. The Battalion was relieved by 10 YORK.R. during the evening & on relief the Battalion moved to Brigade Support at W.23.b. "B" & "D" Companies to W.23.c, one Company "C" in the sunken road W.23.b. "A" Company to Siege Camp & "HQ" to Cavendish Scottish during the line of duty in the front line.	Appx I.12
	11th		A quiet day, visibility was good owing to BRIGHT SUN and day cold. At VAUCELLETTE FARM ashes proceeded as the from line by the Right Brigade (64th) of the Division on the left. Pte Dearman was wounded by shell & 2nd Lieut Wynne-Griffin Officer i/c Rations in Company with 2nd Lieut Bob Lewis from CHAPEL STREET to the trenches. 1st Bn SW Borderers from the Sunk Cheshire Rly X R a32 approximately when the light of the Division was also the Division rly.	6.9
			During the morning Light 4.4 cm & 4.5" field 10.5" em shrapnel fired into the grounds, causing damage west of the Reservoir and the grounds in canvas were mounted into the damage. Bright sunshine visibility good enemy Balloons from...	

A.5834. Wt. W.4973/M687. 750,000. 8/16. D. D. & L. Ltd. Forms/C.2118/13.

WAR DIARY or INTELLIGENCE SUMMARY

Army Form C. 2118.

Place	Date	Hour	Summary of Events and Information	Remarks and references to Appendices
EUDICOURT	January 1918 continued			
	1st	6.30p	The enemy shelled the Battalion area slightly. Two O.R. were killed and 2 O.R. wounded. Nothing of importance to record.	
	2nd		do	
	3rd		do	
	4th		The weather changed during the night.	
	5th		Jan 6/18 rain fell and a thaw followed.	
	8th	8am	Wind South West, from during night, visibility good. The enemy shelled the Brigade area from 4 to 4.45am and dropped heavy shells, at 6am E.A. passed over the sector and dropped a number of bombs.	
			The Battalion relieved the 10th Y.K.R. in the left sub-sector. The relief of the 9th Y.L. which began at 5pm and was completed by 6.30pm. The left of the sub-sector was shown during the relief, but there were no casualties. Disposition in Operation Order by H.R. attached as Appx H. Rain, a little snow during the river continues.	Appx H.
	9th	6am	A draft of 94 O.R. reported from 4th South Lin (Pioneers) having been released by men of a category older than A1.	9G

A5834 Wt. W4973/M687 759,000 8/16 D.D. & L. Ltd. Forms/C2118/13.

Army Form C. 2118.

WAR DIARY
or
INTELLIGENCE SUMMARY.
(Erase heading not required.)

Instructions regarding War Diaries and Intelligence Summaries are contained in F. S. Regs., Part II. and the Staff Manual respectively. Title pages will be prepared in manuscript.

Place	Date	Hour	Summary of Events and Information	Remarks and references to Appendices
HEUDECOURT	10th January 1917	6am	Wind = Westerly, much snow has disappeared and trenches are in a wet state, owing to the thaw.	Appx 5
		5pm	The relief of the front line Companies commenced at 5pm. "D" Company on the right was relieved by "C" Coy. "B" Company on the left was relieved by "A" Coy. Operation order No 43 is attached as Appx 5.	
			Amended Defence Scheme is attached as Appx 6 on the Battalion front.	Appx 6.
	11th	6am	A fairly quiet night. The Railway Embankment in X 13 a was shelled from 5.45am to 6.5am and again at 9am. Corps and Divisional Artillery carried out a bombardment of hostile trenches, and works opposite our front at 6.15am, as far as observation was possible, the shelling was effective, the enemy was fairly quiet throughout the day.	
	12th	6am	A fairly quiet night, enemy shelled ground immediately West of the Railway Embankment X 13 a which 5.9 and H.D shells from 11.5am to 11.R.0 am but did no damage.	JJ

A 5834 Wt. W4973/M687 750,000 8/16 D. D. & L. Ltd. Forms/C.2118/13.

WAR DIARY
or
INTELLIGENCE SUMMARY.

(Erase heading not required.)

Army Form C. 2118.

Place	Date	Hour	Summary of Events and Information	Remarks and references to Appendices
HEUDICOURT	1918 Jan 12th	Wed	Hostile shelling of the Embankment X 13a commenced at 11.25 am and continued till 4 pm. 5.9 shells fell at the rate of 6 or 7 per minute. The hostile shelling was not as though observed as it became erratic at dusk. The Battalion was relieved at dusk by the 10/6 TK.R., the relief was complete by 7.30 pm and the Battalion moved into reserve at RAILWAY CAMP	Appx 4
HEUDECOURT.	13th 14th 15th 16th		The Battalion carried out training and re-organisation	

Lieut. H.W. DICKINSON
Lieut. T. GERTSON
     H. GATESHILL   } 13-1-1918
     G. COPELAND
     F. GOODALL   14.1.1918

Joined the Battalion as reinforcements on the dates stated against their names.

WAR DIARY or INTELLIGENCE SUMMARY

Army Form C. 2118.

Place	Date	Hour	Summary of Events and Information	Remarks and references to Appendices
HEUDECOURT	1918 January 11th	5.30pm	The Battalion relieved 10/York R. in the left Sub-Sector, the leading Company passed H.Q. 10/York.R. at 5.30pm and the relief was complete by 7.30pm. There was a considerable amount of shelling of approaches to trenches from 5.15pm to 7.15pm. One Casualty only. Received Coy Sgt Major CORDUKE'S wounded. O.O. No. 45, Administrative order and Programme for relief attached as Appx 8.	Appx 8.
	14th	6 am	Wind South East — Rain commenced at 8 am from the time the relief was completed all was quiet.	
	18th	6 am to 6	A fairly quiet day, occasional showers wind North West. The usual inter-Company relief commenced at 5.30pm to 7 by relieving "C" Coy on the left and "C" Coy relieving D Company on the right.	
	19th	6 am	Our artillery was active from 5.45 to 6.15 am and it is thought the Artillery belonging to the Division on our left (9 Divn) co-operated. A hostile message intercepted was interpreted as follows "Due 6 o'clock tomorrow morning" Officer Hougin 104 Division (German) fading manual ordered that all if was scared by Brigade to be Known tricky, the necessary arrangements were made to deal with any hostile enterprise	

Army Form C. 2118.

WAR DIARY
or
INTELLIGENCE SUMMARY.
(Erase heading not required.)

Instructions regarding War Diaries and Intelligence Summaries are contained in F. S. Regs., Part II. and the Staff Manual respectively. Title pages will be prepared in manuscript.

Place	Date	Hour	Summary of Events and Information	Remarks and references to Appendices
HEUDECOURT	19th Nov 1916	2pm	There was a considerable amount of hostile shelling between Bn and HQ, the shelling was the direct cause of machine gun Corps teams carrying out a daylight relief in full view of the enemy; so many casualties lost in the opinion of the Infantry the relief by day of Machine Gun Corps is considered infinitely over risk in views of the farmers and visibility good	Appx 9
	20th		The Battalion was relieved by 10th Y & R. K. R. Commencing at 8.30pm the relief was complete at 10.40pm and the Battalion moved into Brigade support with Bn. H.Q. and three Coys in the Railway Embankment at W 23 b. and one Coy at 7 E 7, 1 E. R. G. S. Lieut. H. N. JACKSON was killed whilst employed with 94th Coy R E.	
	21st 22nd 23rd		Training in Anti gas devise, Working parties and whilst possible cleaning clothing, arms and S.A.A.	2JY

A.5834 Wt. W4973/M687 750,000 8/16 D. D. & L. Ltd. Forms/C.2118/13.

WAR DIARY
or
INTELLIGENCE SUMMARY.
(Erase heading not required.)

Army Form C. 2118.

Place	Date 1918	Hour	Summary of Events and Information	Remarks and references to Appendices
HEUDICOURT	Jan 24th	—	The Battalion relieved 10/York & Lancs Regt in the Left Sub-Sector commencing at 4.15 p.m. The Battalion was disposed as follows:— Right: D Company Left: B Company Support: C Company Counter-attack: A Company	
	25th		The relief was complete at 8.30 p.m. Things were quiet until mid-day. Enemy shelled the Railway Embankment with shell bursts from 5.9 and 4.2 guns during the afternoon. At 4.30 p.m. and 11 p.m. the enemy shelled the Battalion area with gas-shells (Phosgene), about 40 to 80 shells were used each time and two casualties only resulted, one from a splinter M shell and a N.C.O. (who was standing near the place struck by a gas shell) who was unaware that gas shells were being used. A patrol of 1 Officer (Lieut. B.F. ASTBURY) and six O.R. went our from the Right Company area and did not return, there was a considerable amount of M.G. and air "Strad L."	Appx 10 {G.O. No 48 {administration Appx 10
	26th		Foggy, some M.Gun fire during the night and an "Strad L."	

A5834 Wt W4973/M687 750,000 8/16 D.D.&L. Ltd. Forms/C.2118/13.

WAR DIARY or INTELLIGENCE SUMMARY

Army Form C. 2118.

Place	Date	Hour	Summary of Events and Information	Remarks and references to Appendices
HEUDECOURT	26th	—	The relief of B.W. Corps in the front line by the Support and Counter-attacking Companies took place at 5.30 p.m. B Coy moved into the area occupied by the Counter-attacking Company and D Company into Support. O.O. No HQ is attached as Appendix 11.	Appx. 11.
	27th		Officers of 16th R. Rifle Bde visited the Battalion for the purpose of reconnoitring the trenches prior to the taking over of the sector by the 39th Division.	
	28th		The Battalion was relieved by 10th O.R.K.R. commencing at 9.15 p.m., during the relief about 50 gas shells fell in the vicinity of Battalion H.Q. 20 casualties received. The relief was complete by 10.15 p.m. and the Battalion moved into Brigade Reserve at RAILWAY and MIDDLESEX CAMPS HEUDECOURT. Operation Order No 50 and Administrative Orders as attached as Appendix 12.	Appx. 12.
	29th 30th	→ →	The day was spent in cleaning up and re-organizing Coys into 4 Platoon The Battalion moved from HEUDECOURT by Light Railway in three parties to MOISLAINS.	
	30th		Training and re-organization was carried out under Company Commanders.	

Capt 13th? M? No 165 Signed E.C. Graham

Appx. 1

OPERATION ORDER NO. 43.   SECRET
--------------------------   1.1.17
Ref. Map 57c S.E.   Copy No. 2

1. RELIEF.
   BEAR will be relieved by TIGRESS on the evening of 2nd Jan.
   as follows:
   "A" Coy TIGRESS will relieve "A" Coy BEAR on the Left.
   "B"   do   do   "B" do   in Reserve.
   "C"   do   do   "C" do   on the Right.
   "D"   do   do   "D" do   in Support.

   BEAR on relief will take up position of Bde Reserve,
   H.Q. and 3 Coys in Railway Embankment N.25.b. and one Coy
   in Sunken Road N.30.a.9.0.

2. ADVANCED PARTIES.
   Advanced Parties from B. C. & D.Coys and H.Q. TIGRESS
   will be at Bn.H.Q. BEAR by 2-30.p.m. 2nd. inst. Advance Party of
   A. Company TIGRESS will be at Bn.H.Q. BEAR by 6 a.m. 2nd. inst.
   Advanced Parties from Coys and H.Q. BEAR will consist of
   1 Officer. 1. N.C.O. and 1. Runner and will report at
   TIGRESS H.Q. in Railway Embankment N.25.b. by 2.p.m. 2nd. inst.

3. GUIDES.
   2.Guides per Coy from A and C. Coys BEAR and 1.Guide per
   Coy from B. and D. Coys BEAR will be at Bn.H.Q. by 4-45.p.m.
   to meet the relieving Coys, which will arrive in order.
   "A",   "C",   "B",   "D".

4. STORES.
   All Grenades, S.A.A., S.O.S. Signals, Tools, Defence
   Schemes etc, will be handed over.   Coys will forward to
   Bn.H.Q. by 9.a.m. 2nd inst, List of Stores they will be
   handing over and by 10.a.m. 3rd, receipts for Stores
   handed over.

   ADMINISTRATIVE ORDERS will be issued later.

5. COMPLETION OF RELIEF.
   Completion of relief will be notified to Bn.H.Q. by code
   word "SNOWDON"

                Copy No.1.   Bde.
                     2.   C.O.
                     3.   TIGRESS.
                     4.   A. Coy.
                     5.   B. "
                     6.   C. "
                     7.   D. "
                     8.   T.O.
                     9.   Q.M.

                                      C. O. Lacey.
                                      .... 2nd. Lieut.
                                           Adjt.   B E A R.

Appendix 2

12/13th NORTHUMBERLAND FUSILIERS

ADMINISTRATIVE ORDERS
TO ACCOMPANY OPERATION ORDER
No 52.
17.9.18

1. The A/Q.M will remain at the present Camp to hand over all Tents, Camp Equipment etc.

2. ADVANCED PARTIES.
A/R.Q.M.S, 1 N.C.O and 1 Man per Company will parade at Orderly Room at 8 a.m to go forward to new Camp.
Capt. J.R. SHORT will march this party.

3. CAMP EQUIPMENT.
No Camp equipment will be removed, all beds, forms etc will be handed over on relief.

4. OFFICERS KITS etc
Officers Kits will be at Q.M. Stores by 9.30 a.m. Mess Boxes will be at Battn H.Q. at 10 a.m

5. BLANKETS.
Blankets will be rolled in bundles of ten, labelled and placed at loading point D.29.c.4.6. One N.C.O per Coy will remain in charge.

6. CAPS.
All Service dress Caps will be collected and placed on Transport.

7. LORRIES.
Three Lorries will be reporting at CHURCH, TEMPLEUX la FOSSE at 12 noon. Guide will meet lorries and guide them to loading point.

(sd) J.W. ELLIOTT
2nd Lieut.
Actg Adjutant 12/13th Northumberland Fusiliers

Appx 2.

BEAR
ADMINISTRATIVE ORDER.

1.1.18

1. **RELIEF.** On relief "A", "B", "C" and "D" Coys BEAR will take over positions occupied by respective Coys of TIGRESS. A, B & D & HQ in Rly Embankment W.23.b. & C Coy in Sunken Rd W.30. a.9.0.

2. **GUIDES.** The Runners from the Advanced Parties BEAR will report back to the present Bn H.Q. by 5 p.m. tomorrow to conduct Coys to their respective positions.

3. **TRANSPORT.** T.O. will arrange for the Mess Cart and 2 Limber Wagons to be at present Bn H.Q. immediately after dark tomorrow for Mess Boxes, Officers trench kits etc.
    Mess Boxes and Officers trench kits etc. will be outside Bn H.Q. by 4.45 p.m.
    Lewis Gunners will carry their Lewis Guns out.
    Rations for 3rd Jan. will be brought to New Battn H.Q. in Railway Embankment W.23.b.
    The three Cookers will come up to the Railway Embankment W.23.b. by 4 p.m. tomorrow, to cook for A, B, D and H.Q.Coys.
    Cooking for "C" Coy will be done in Dixies in the SUNKEN ROAD W.30.a.9.0, where there are petrol tins and a water tank to keep the water supply.
    Water carts will come up filled by 4 p.m. tomorrow; one to C Coy cookhouse and one to the Railway Embankment to fill up dixies and water tanks etc. They will do another journey tomorrow night and from the 3rd inst until further notice, will do three journeys per day to maintain the supply.
    Coys will arrange for their ration parties & cooks to carry their dixies to their new cookhouses by 4 p.m. tomorrow in order to prepare Dinners for A & C Coys and teas for B and D Coys when they arrive.

4. **WORKING PARTIES.** Working parties of 1 N.C.O. and 30 men will be detailed to report to 178th Tunnelling Coy R.E. at VAUDRICOURT FARM as follows:
    B Coy   4 p.m.   2nd Jan.
    do.   12 m/n   2/3rd Jan.
    D Coy   8 a.m.   3rd Jan.
    A party of 12 men for work with 178th Tunnelling Coy R.E. near LEFT Bn H.Q. will be detailed by D Coy. They will work in shifts as follows:
    Four men from 4 p.m. 2nd to m/n 2/3rd Jan.
    do   m/n 2/3rd to 8 a.m. 3rd Jan.
    do   8 a.m. 3rd to 4 p.m. 3rd.
    They should be conducted by a N.C.O.

5. COMPANY Commanders of A, B, & D Coys will report personally to Commanding Officer on arrival into new position. "C" Coy will report by wire.

6. THE Commanding Officer will see Coy Commanders at Bn H.Q. at 9.30 a.m. on the 3rd inst.

C.W.Lacey
.... 2nd Lieut.
A/Adjt BEAR

Orders.

Appx 3.

DEFENCE ARRANGEMENTS

SUPPORT BATTALION

IN case of alarm
1. (a) The Battn will stand to arms.
   (b) The Coy detailed to occupy the BROWN LINE will move off at once and report to Battn H.Q. immediately the allotted posts have been occupied.
   (c) The Coy Commanders of other Coys will inform Battn H.Q. as soon as their Coys are ready to move.
2. The Battn (less Coy detailed to occupy the BROWN LINE) will be prepared either
   (a) to counter-attack on any part of the Brigade front, or
   (b) Reinforce the BROWN LINE
3. A telephone line will be laid from Battn H.Qn to the H.Q. of the Coy in the BROWN LINE
4. The Coy detailed to occupy the BROWN LINE will be prepared to move at 15 minutes notice between the hours of 6 a.m. & 8 a.m. and 3 p.m. and 6 p.m. daily.

.... Lieut Col.
Comdg.t B E A R.

3.1.18

Appx H

BEAR   SECRET

OPERATION ORDER NO. 43

Ref. Map
Sh.57c.S.E.

7.1.18
Copy No........

1. **RELIEF.** The Battalion will relieve the 10th YORKSHIRE RGT. tomorrow 8th inst.
    Coys will leave their present areas in time to pass the H.Q. 10th Yorkshire R. as follows:-
    D Coy - 5 p.m.   A Coy   5.10 p.m.
    B "   5.5 p.m.   C "   5.15 p.m.
            H.Q. 5.30 p.m.
    B & C Coys will cross this railway Embankment by the Eastern end, A & D Coys by the Western End.
    An interval of at least 500 yards will be maintained between Coys.
    No guides will be required.

2. **DISPOSITIONS.**
    6, 7 & 8 Posts   D Coy
    9 & 10   "   B "
    Counterattacking Coy   A Coy.
    Reserve Coy   C "
    One Lewis-Gun will be found from A Coy for the detached post at X.7.d.2.2 and will come under the orders of the Left Coy.
    Corresponding Coys 10th Yorkshire Regt will be occupying these positions.

3. **ADVANCED PARTIES.** An Advanced party from B Coy will report at the Coy H.Q. Left Coy at 6 a.m. tomorrow. Password:- ANDREW.
    Advanced Parties from H.Q., A, C, & D Coys will report at H.Q. to which their Coys are going at 2 p.m.
        Strength:- 1 Officer
                   1 Sergeant
                   1 O.R. per Platoon.
    Advanced parties of 3/4th The Queens (R.W.S.) Regt will arrive at Support Bn H.Q. at 2 p.m.

4. **STORES.** All stores etc. will be taken over and list of same rendered to Bn H.Q. by 9 a.m.

5. **COMMUNICATION.** The Left Coy will by means of a code-word notify Coy H.Q. every hour that all is correct in the forward area.

6. **GUM BOOTS.** Gum boots for front line Coys have been applied for.

7. **COMPLETION OF RELIEF.** Completion of relief will be notified by code word "PERCY".

8. **WORK.** The Counterattacking Coy:
        1 Platoon will wire in front of the right support trench
        1 Platoon will work on ARC SUPPORT.
    The Reserve Coy:
        1 Platoon will wire CAVALRY LINE
        1   "   "   widen C.T. between 7 & 8 Posts.

9. **STAND-TO.** 6 a.m. to Daylight
                  3.45 p.m. to 5 p.m.

- 2 -

10. WORKING PARTIES. C Coy will supply Working Party of 1 N.C.O. and 30 men for work with Tunnelling Coy R.E. near Right Bn H.Q. at 8 a.m. tomorrow instead of D Coy. They will parade in full marching order with all rations and on being relieved proceed to the new area.

    3/4th The Queens (RWS) Rgt will take over Working parties with 178th Tunnelling Coy R.E. from 4 p.m. 8th inst.

11. ADMINISTRATIVE INSTRUCTIONS will be issued later.

............................2nd Lieut.
A/Adjt 12/13th Northd Fusiliers.

ISSUED BY ORDERLY
AT 4.45 p.m.

No.	Copy	
1	"	Brigade
2	"	C.O.
3	"	File
4	"	10 Yorkshire R.
5	"	A Coy
6	"	B
7	"	C
8	"	D
9	"	T.O.
10	"	Q.M.
11	"	R.S.M.

ADMINISTRATIVE INSTRUCTIONS

Appx 4.

7.1.18

1. **TRANSPORT.** The T.O. will arrange for the Mess Cart to be at present Bn H.Q. by 4.30 p.m. tomorrow for Mess Boxes. And 2 Limber wagons to report after delivering Rations for Officers Trench Kits and Dixies.

   Mess Boxes, Officers Trench kits and Dixies will be outside Bn H.Q. by 4.30 p.m. At least one man per Coy must accompany the above to be responsible for loading and unloading.

   Rations for the 9th will be delivered to the new Bn H.Q. <u>after dusk</u>. Water carts will come up filled, <u>after dusk</u>, and will do two further journeys.

2. **COOKING ARRANGEMENTS.** Cooking arrangements and meals will be the same as during the last tour of duty. Teas tomorrow will be served before Coys move off.

3. **R.E. MATERIAL.** R.E. Material will be drawn from Dump at Bn H.Q. Indents as usual.

4. **SALVAGE.** The Bn Salvage Party will continue to work, and live at Battn H.Q. Coys will send in Salvage to Bn Dump each day.

5. **WORK.** D Coy will work in CAVALRY Support trench tomorrow.

G W Lacey ....2nd Lieut
A/Adjt 12/13th Northd Fusrs.

OPERATION ORDER NO. 43　Appx 5　SECRET
10.1.18

1. RELIEF. "A" Coy will relieve "B" Coy in the LEFT Coy area tonight.
"C" Coy will relieve "D" Coy in the RIGHT Coy area tonight.
The relief will commence at 5 p.m. at which time relieving Coys will leave their present quarters.
Completion of relief will be notified to H.Q. by the Coy Commanders being relieved, they will report personally.
All details of work proposed will be handed over and as litt-le delay as possible will be caused by the relief.
Care must be taken that no indication of a relief is given to the enemy.
Detached Lewis Gun Post occupied by "A" Coy will be relieved by "B" Coy.

2. MEALS. "A" & "C" Coys will have tea before they move off. "B" & "D" Coys will have dinners when they get back into position.
Coys will have the same arrangements for meals as the Coys they relieve.

3. STORES. All stores as stated in O.O. No. 42 will be handed over.

G.W. Lacey

...................2nd Lieut.
A/Adjt B E A R.

To: A ~~Coy~~, B, C, D Coys.

Appx 6

SECRET

B E A R

DEFENCE SCHEME.

LEFT SUB-SECTOR
of
LEFT BRIGADE.

1. BOUNDARIES (a) On the right - X.14.a.0.2 X.13.central - railway at X.13.c.9.9.
   (b) On the left - CHAPEL STREET (north Brigade Boundary).
   (c) "LION" are on our right and the 9th Division on our left.

2. DISPOSITIONS. (a) Battn H.Q. - Western side of Railway embankment at X.13.a.2.5.
   (b) Front line - Two companies.
   RIGHT COY. H.Q. in BIRCHTREE COPSE X.13.b.2.2.
   No. 6 Post - 1 Lewis Gun section and 2 rifle sections in RACKET TRENCH from X.13.b.35.10 to X.13.b.35.30
   No. 7 Post - 1 Lewis Gun section and 1 Rifle section in RACKET TRENCH from X.13.b.35.35 to X.13.b.3.5.
   No. 8 Post - 2 Lewis Gun sections in RACKET TRENCH from X.13.b.40.85 to X.7.d.46.05
   This company has its own support of one Rifle section (15 men) which occupies TENNIS TRENCH from X.13.a.40.05 to X.13.a.35.60 at morning "Stand-to" and immediately at any time an alarm is given.

   1st platoon

   LEFT COY. Coy H.Q. at X.7.c.15.30
   No. 9 Post - 1 Lewis Gun section and 2 rifle sections in FIVES TRENCH from X.7.d.45.50 to X.7.d.3.8
   No.10 Post - 2 Lewis gun sections and one rifle section in FIVES TRENCH from X.7.d.5.8 to X.7.d.40.85
   This company has a support of one Lewis gun section and one rifle section which occupy ARC TRENCH from X.7.c.2.1 to X.7.c.3.4 at morning "Stand-to" and immediately, at any time, in the event of alarm.
   (c) SUPPORT. One company.
   Coy H.Q. X.13.a.15.65.
   At morning "Stand-to" and in the event of alarm, this company holds two 1-platoon posts in the CAVALRY TRENCH
   Right post from X.13.a.05.10 to W.18.b.9.1, and Left post from W.18.b.50.45 to W.18.b.35.45.
   The garrison for the Right post live at present in shelters on W. side of Railway X.13.a, and of the Left post in shelters in SUNKEN ROAD about W.18.b.2.5.00

   (d) COUNTER ATTACKING COY. are in shelters on Western side of Railway embankment X.13.a. Coy H.Q. X.13.a.2.8
   Counter attacking Coy finds a detached Lewis Gun post permanently at X.7.d.25.30

   (e) OBSERVATION POST - X.7.c.15.35

- 1 -

- 2 -

3. **ALTERATIONS OF DISPOSITIONS.**
    (a) Battalion H.Q. will move to W.18.c.8.5 as soon as tunnelled dugouts there has been completed. It is not likely to be ready for 2 or 3 weeks.
    (b) Support Coy. Coy H.Q. and 1 Platoon will move from Railway embankment X.13.a. to SUNKEN ROAD about W.18.b.6.1 as soon as dugouts have been completed.
    (c) On completion of (b) the Right Front line Coy H.Q. will move to positions vacated by Support Coy at X.13.a.15.65

4. **COMMUNICATION.** LEFT Coy forward posts are connected with LEFT Coy H.Q.; all Coy H.Q. with Battn H.Q., and Battn H.Q. with BOLT by wire.

5. **DEFENCE.**
    (a) <u>Action in case of attack.</u>
        The whole Battalion will "stand-to".
    (b) The front line will be held at all costs.
    (c) The Support Coy will hold the CAVALRY TRENCH as stated in "2 (c)".
    (d) The Counter-attacking Coy will be ready, without waiting for further orders, either:-
        1. To counter-attack in order to recover the front line.
        2. To man the support trenches just EAST of the Railway embankment.
    (e) The garrisons detailed from front line Coys to hold ARC TRENCH and TENNIS TRENCH will not move forward with counter-attacking troops.
    (f) Coys will keep Battn H.Q. informed at once of the progress of events, and of all action taken.

6. **R.A. POST** - Railway X.13.a.2.5.

7. **S.A.A. GRENADES ETC.** Dumps are at Battn & Coy H.Qs.

8. **S.O.S.** (a) The signal now in use is two green and two white lights fired by means of a Rifle Grenade.
    (b) When the S.O.S. Signal is put up all Batteries on the Divisional front will open fire for 5 minutes, and then stop unless the signal is repeated, and unless it is clear that a serious attack is in progress. If the S.O.S. signal is sent up between 6 a.m. and 8 a.m. fire will be kept up for 15 minutes without further instructions.
    (c) Two rifles, fixed in racks, for firing S.O.S. rockets - loaded with blank cartridges, and with the grenade rod in them are at Battn H.Q., each Coy H.Q. & No. 9 Post. The grenades are kept in tins close by.

...........................Major
Cmdg 12/13th Nortbd Fusrs.

9.1.18

Appx 4.

OPERATION ORDER NO. 44   SECRET
----------------------------   11.1.18

Copy No. ......

1. **RELIEF.** 10th Yorkshire Regt will relieve 12/13th Northumberland Fus. in the LEFT sub-sector tomorrow evening 12th. Corresponding Coys will be relieving.

    Coys, 10th Yorkshire Regt. will arrive at Battn H.Q. and put on Gum boots, as follows:-

    RIGHT Coy   5.30 p.m.
    LEFT "   5.45 p.m.
    SUPPORT   6.0 p.m.
    RESERVE   6.5 p.m.

    12/13th Northd Fusrs. will take up position of Bde Reserve in MIDDLESEX and RAILWAY CAMPS, HEUDECOURT.

    On arrival at HEUDECOURT Coys will take over Billets of Coys of 10th Yorkshire R. as follows:-

    C Coy 12/13th Northd Fus, billets of C Coy 10th Yorks R
    D "   "   "   "   A "   "
    B "   "   "   "   B "   "
    A "   "   "   "   D "   "

    C & D Coys will occupy the TUNNEL.

    On relief all Gum-boots will be handed in at Bn H.Q. and receipts obtained. A N.C.O. should be detailed for the duty of receiving them.

    No guides will be required.

2. **ADVANCED PARTIES.** Advanced party of 10th Yorkshire R. for LEFT Coy will arrive at 6 a.m. tomorrow. Advanced Parties for remainder of Coys at 4 p.m. tomorrow.

    Party to take over drying room and Gum-boots will arrive at 4 p.m. tomorrow.

    Major A.E.SCOTT and 2nd Lieut. J.W.ELLIOTT will proceed to the Camp at HEUDECOURT at 9 a.m. tomorrow to take over huts and allot accomodation.

    Major Scott will ascertain what the defence arrangements are and notify Coy Commanders concerned.

    Transport Officer will arrange for:-
    The Party from the 14th Bn Northd Fus, shoemakers, Tailors, Barbers and Nucleus Party to be at HEUDECOURT at 2.30 p.m. tomorrow.

3. **STORES.** All stores etc. will be handed over. Coys will forward to Bn H.Q. by 10 a.m. 13th inst. list of stores handed over.

4. **COMPLETION OF RELIEF.** Completion of Relief will be notified by code-word "JONES".

    FURTHER ADMINISTRATIVE INSTRUCTIONS will be issued later.

..................................2nd Lieut.
A/Adjt 12/13th Northd Fusrs.

Copy No. 1 Brigade   Copy No. 6 C Coy
         2 C.O.   7 D
         3 10th Yorkshire R.   8 T.O.
         4 A Coy   9 Q.M.
         5 B "   10 R.S.M.

Appx 8.   SECRET

OPERATION ORDER NO. 45

Copy No. 3
15.1.18

Ref. Map 57C S.E.
1/20.000.

1. **RELIEF.** The Battn will relieve 10th Bn Yorkshire R. in Left Sub-sector of Brigade front tomorrow 16th inst., Coys relieving corresponding letter Coys of 10th Yorkshire R.
    Coys will move off in time to pass H.Q. of 10th Yorkshire R. as follows:
    D Coy   5.30 p.m.   RIGHT Coy front line.
    B "   5.40 "   LEFT   do
    H.Q.   5.50 "
    A Coy   6.0- "   Counter-attacking Coy
    C "   6.10 "   Support Coy.
    Coys will march by platoons with 5 minutes interval.
    Dress: full marching order, leather jerkins will be worn.
    Guides: No guides will be required.

2. **DISPOSITIONS.** One half SUPPRT Coy & Coy H.Q. are in dugouts in Sunken Road in W.18.b.6.1.
    1 Lewis Gun from Counterattacking Coy will be attached to LEFT front line Coy for tactical purposes.

3. **ADVANCED PARTY.** 2nd Lieut. J.W.ELLIOTT, C.S.M.Dawson and 2 Runners from Battn H.Q. will go forward to take over reporting at H.Q. 10th Yorkshire R. at 2 p.m.

4. **LEWIS GUNS ETC.** Lewis Guns will be conveyed by Transport to Battn H.Q. and be stacked by Coys under 1 Lewis Gun N.C.O. per Coy to be collected by Coys as they pass Bn H.Q. L.G.O. to arrange.
    Transport Officer will arrange for wagon for Officers Trench kits to be at Battn H.Q. at 4.30 p.m.
    Officers Mess kit will be at Bn H.Q. by 5 p.m. to be taken to trenches.

5. **TRENCH STORES.** All trench stores etc. will be taken over and lists sent to Orderly Room by 9 a.m. on 17th inst.

6. **COMPLETION OF RELIEF.** Completion of relief will be notified to Bn H.Q. by code word "ALGY".

7. **ADMINISTRATIVE ORDERS.** Administrative orders and programme of work will be issued later.

8. **ACKNOWLEDGE.**

.... Capt.
Adjt 12/13th Northd Fusiliers.

Copy No. 1 Brigade   No. 6 B Coy
         2 10th Yorkshire R.   7 C
         3 C.O.   8 D
         4 File   9 T.O.
         5 A Coy   10 Q.M.
                                 11 R.S.M.

ADMINISTRATIVE ORDERS.

1. **TRANSPORT.** Q.M.Stores and Transport Lines will remain at present location.

2. **COOKING, WATER.** Cooking arrangements will be as when previously in the LEFT Sub-sector. T.O. will arrange for transport to convey Dixies etc. to Railway embankment and arrange for Water carts to come up each evening.

3. **RATIONS.** Rations will be dumped at Bn H.Q. each evening commencing tomorrow 16th inst.

4. **NUCLEUS PARTY.** Nucleus party made up as follows will be left at Transport Lines:
   Officers as already detailed.
   8 Signallers trained from Bn H.Q.
   7   "   untrained from Coys.
       Above to be detailed by S.O.
   2 partially trained L. Gunners per Coy.
   Sick men up to 6# per Coy to be detailed by Coy Cmdrs
       on recommendation of M.O.
   Sgt MURPGY "A" Coy as physical Instructor.
    " WESTGARTH L.G.Sergeant
    " SHAW   Bombing Sergeant.

5. **DETAILS FOR TRANSPORT LINES.** The Nucleus Party, as above, details for transport lines, N.C.Os. and men proceeding on Courses, and O.Rs. proceeding on leave on 19th inst. will parade at 3.30 p.m. under Lieut. DICKINSON opposite B Coy Hut.

6. **BLANKETS.** Blankets rolled in Bundles of 10 and labelled will be stacked by Coys at entrance to Coy huts and collected by Transport at 11 a.m.

7. **BILLETS.** O.C. Coys will inspect Coy Billets (Huts and Tunnel) before moving off from camp.

8. **RETURNS.** While in the Line returns will be as per list previously issued with the addition of "Return of Intended Patrols" due at Bn H.Q. at 12 noon daily.

9. **PROGRAMME OF WORK.** The Programme of Work while in the line is attached.
   Work is under supervision of a R.E. Officer.

................................2nd Lieut.
A/Adjt 12/13th Northd Fusrs.

15.1.18

ADMINISTRATIVE ORDERS.

1. MEALS. All meals will be issued tomorrow 20th inst. before the relief takes place.

2. COOKING ARRANGEMENTS. Cooks and Ration parties will carry cooking utensils to new positions.
   Cooking arrangements will be the same as when Battn was previously in Brigade Support.

3. RATIONS, WATER. Rations for 21st inst will be taken to new positions. Water carts will come up to new positions tomorrow night 20th inst. and water supply arrangements will be as when previously in Bde Support.

4. OFFICERS MESS BOXES, TRENCH KITS. T.O. will arrange for the Mess cart and 2 limbers wagons to be at Bn H.Q. at 9 p.m. tomorrow for Mess boxes, Officers trench kits etc. Mess boxes & kits will be at Bn Dump at that time; 1 Servant per Coy will be left in charge.

..................Captain
Adjt. BEAR.

19.1.18

PROGRAMME OF WORK.

Counter-attacking Coy and Support Coy work in front line under R.E. from 8.30 a.m. to 3.30 p.m. daily.
Dinners at 3.30 p.m.
1 Officer of each of the above Coys will report to R.E. Officer at RIGHT Coy H.Q. at 8.15 a.m. daily.

Garrison of front line work from 7.30 p.m. to 11.30 p.m. and 12.30 a.m. to 6 a.m. daly.
1 Officer from each front line Coy will report to R.E. Officers at 7.15 p.m. at RIGHT Coy H.Q.

G.W. Lacey 2nd Lieut.
A/Adjt 12/13th Northd Fusiliers.

15.1.18.

Appx 9.

OPERATION ORDER NO. 47   SECRET

Ref. Map. 57C S.E.   Copy No...3...
1/20.000.

1. RELIEF. The Bn will be relieved by correspondinly
   lettered Coys of 10th Bn YORKSHIRE R. on the evening of
   the 20th inst. as follows:
   "C" Coy 10th Yorks. R. RIGHT Coy pass Bn H.Q. 8.30 p.m.
   "A"   - do   LEFT   do   8.40 p.m.
   "B"   do   COUNTER- ATTACKING)
                         COY.   ) do 8.50 p.m.
   "D"   do   SUPPORT Coy   do 9.0 p.m.
         On relief Bn will go into Brigade Support, Coys will
   take over the positions previously occupied.
         A, B & D Coys & H.Q. in Railway Embankment W.23.b.
   and C Coy in Sunken Road W.30.a.9.0.

2. GUIDES. No guides will be required.

3. ADVANCED PARTIES. There will be no advanced parties from
   10th Yorkshire R. for Coys.
         An Advanced Party of 1 Officer & 1 Sergeant per Coy
   and Bn H.Q. will go forward to take over respective
   positions from 10th Yorkshire R. but parties will not
   leave trenches till after dusk.

4. GUM BOOTS. All Gum boots will be taken out by Coys.

5. LEWIS GUNS. B & D Coys will carry out Lewis Guns etc. to
   new positions. Lewis Guns of A & C Coys will be brought
   to Bn Dump and loaded on Transport. 1 L.G. N.C.O.,
   per Coy will remain with Coy Guns.

6. STORES. All grenades, S.A.A., S.O.S., Signals, Tools
   defence schemes, etc. will be handed over and receipts
   for stores handed over forwarded to Bn H.Q. by 10 a.m.
   21st inst.
         Tools will be collected at Coy dumps.

7. COMPLETION OF RELIEF. Completion of relief will be
   notified to Bn H.Q. by code word "ROBERT".

8. ADMINISTRATIVE ORDERS ETC. Administrative orders,
   Programme of Work while in Bde Support & Defence
   Arrangements are issued separately.

9. A C K N O W L E D G E.

                              ....Captain
                              Adjt B E A R.

ISSUED BY ORDERLY
AT 5.30 p.m.
   19.1.18

            Copy No. 1 Bde
                     2 10th Yorkshire R.
                     3 C.O.
                     4 File
                     5 A Coy
                     6 B
                     7 C
                     8 D
                     9 T.O.
                    10 Q.M.
                    11 R.S.M.

Ref. Map
57C S.E.
1/20.000

OPERATION ORDER NO. m48

App. 10.

SECRET
Copy No...... 2
23.1.18

1. RELIEF. The Battn will relieve the 10th Yorkshire R. in the Left sub-sector of the Brigade front on the evening of the 24th inst., Coys relieving correspondingly lettered Coys of 10th Yorkshire R. as follows:-

    D. Coy RIGHT Coy pass Bn H.Q. 10 Yorks R. at 7.15 p.m.
    B " LEFT do do 7.25 p.m.
    A " COUNTERATTACK do 7.35 p.m.
    C " SUPPORT do do 7.45 p.m.
    H.Q. do do 7.30 p.m.

No guides will be required. 1 Lewis Gun of A Coy will be attached to B Coy for tactical purposes.

2. ADVANCED PARTY. 2/Lieut. J.W.ELLIOTT, A/R.S.M. and 4 O.Rs. from Battn H.Q. will report at Battn H.Q. 10th Yorks R. at 5.30 p.m. to take over Stores etc.

3. LEWIS GUNS, TRENCH KITS ETC. Lewis Guns will be carried in by Coys.
T.O. will arrange for the Mess Cart and 2 Limbers for Officers Trench kits etc. to be at Battn H.Q. at 6.30 p.m. Mess boxes, trench kits etc. will be at Battn H.Q. at that time. 1 Servant per company will remain in charge.
T.O. will also arrange for 1 limber for dixes and cooks Stores to be at Battn H.Q. at 5.30 p.m.

4. GUM BOOTS. All gum boots will be taken into trenches. Coys proceeding to front line will wear Gum boots and carry ankle boots.

5. TRENCH STORES. All grenades S.A.A., S.O.S, Signals, Tools etc. will be taken over and lists of stores taken over forwarded to Battn H.Q. by 10 a.m. on 25th inst.

6. INCOMING UNIT. The 3/4 The Queens (RWS) R. are taking over positions at present occupied by the Battn. Advanced parties will be reporting at Coy H.Q. during afternoon of 24th inst.

7. ADMINISTRATIVE ORDERS. Administrative Orders and Programme of Work will be issued later.

8. COMPLETION OF RELIEF. Completion of relief will be notified to Battn H.Q. by code word "PERCY".

9. A C K N O W L E D G E.

                    ....Captain
                    Adjt 12/13th Northd Fusiliers.

ISSUED BY ORDERLY
AT 5 p.m.

Copy No. 1 Brigade
2 C.O.
3 10th Yorks R.
4 A Coy
5 B
6 C
7 D
9 T.O.
10 Q.M.
11 A/R.S.M.

ADMINISTRATIVE ORDERS.

1. COOKING AND WATER. The cooking arrangements will be the same as when the Battn was previously in the LEFT subsector.
   Cooks and ration carrying party will proceed with cooks wagon to cookhouses in new area to be there by 6.30 p.m. to prepare usual hot meal for issue during the night.

2. RATIONS. Rations will be taken up to Battn H.Q. each night commencing tomorrow 24th inst.

3. RETURNS. Returns required from Coys while in trenches will be the same as before with following alterations "Indent for R.E. Stores due at 8.30 a.m. daily" instead of 1 p.m. "Intended Patrols due at 8.30 p.m. daily" instead of 12 noon.

4. S.O.S. SIGNALS. The new S.O.S. Signals to be used is a rifle grenade signal which bursts into 4 lights - 2 red and 2 green. This will be repeated until artillery complies.

5. PROGRAMME OF WORK. Programme of working parties to be found while in the line will be issued later.

..................Captain
Adjt. 12/13th Northd Fusrs.

23.1.18

Ref Map
57C S.E.
1/20.000

OPERATION ORDER NO 49 Appx II

SECRET
Copy No 1

1. RELIEF.   The following inter company reliefs will take place on the night of 26th inst.
   A Coy will relieve B Coy in LEFT Coy area of Bn Front
   C   do   D do RIGHT   do
   Relief will commence at 8.30 p.m.
   1 Lewis Gun of B Coy will remain under orders of O.C. A Coy for tactical purposes.
   On relief B Coy will occupy present position of A Coy
   and D   do   do   C

2. STORES.   All trench stores, details of work proposed etc. will be handed over.

3. MEALS.   All meals will be issued to Coys before relief commences.
   The evening hot meal will be issued at usual time.

4. WORKING PARTIES. The Carrying parties for R.E. at 5.30 p.m. will be supplied as usual tomorrow evening by A and C Coys.

5. COMPLETION OF RELIEF. Completion of relief will be notified to Bn H.Q. by O.C. B & D Coys personally.

   A C K N O W L E D G E.

   ....Captain
   Adjt BEAR

25.1.18

AMENDMENT TO OPERATION ORDER NO. 49   SECRET
--   Copy No. 1

Reference para. 1. RELIEF.
For "Relief will commence at 8.30 p.m" substitute
   Relief will commence at 5.30 p.m.

Cancel para. 3. MEALS., and substitute
   "A & C Coys will have teas before marching off
   "B & D   "   will have dinners on arrival in new positions"

Cancel para. 4. WORKING PARTIES., and substitute   at midnight tonight
   "The carrying parties for R.E. will be found at ~~8.30 p.m.~~
   "by B & D Coys. Officers in charge of parties will
   "report at Battn H.Q. at 8.25 p.m."

                                    ....Captain
                                         Adjt. B E A R.

26.1.18

Appendix No.12.

OPERATION ORDER NO 50   SECRET
                         Copy No ___3___

Ref Map
57C S E
1/20,000

1. RELIEF.   The Battn will be relieved by correspondingly
   lettered Coys of the 10th YORKSHIRE R. on the evening
   of the 28th inst.
          The leading Coy of the 10th Yorkshire R. will
   pass Battn H.Q. at ~~5.30 p.m.~~ 9.15pm
          No guides will be required.
          On relief the Battn will go into Brigade Reserve
   at HEUDICOURT.

2. ADVANCED PARTIES.   There will be no advanced parties from
   the 10th Yorks R. Major G.WHITE, M.C. and a party from
   Bn H.Q. will go forward to take over RAILWAY CAMP on
   the 28th inst.

3. STORES.   All trench stores, defence schemes etc. will
   be handed over and receipts obtained.   Lists of stores
   handed over will be forwarded to Orderly Room by 10 a.m.
   on 29th inst.

4. MEALS.   A & C Coys will have dinner on arrival at
   HEUDICOURT.
          B &D Coys & H.Q. will have meals at usual times.

5. LEWIS GUNS, OFFICERS KITS ETC.   T.O. will arrange for
   2 Lewis Gun wagons to be at Bn H.Q. at 5.30 p.m.
   to collect Lewis Guns.   Coys except D Coy will stack
   Lewis Guns by Coys at Bn Dump under 1 Lewis Gun N.C.O.
   per Company.   Lewis Guns of D Coy will be collected
   at a place to be selected by the L.G.O.
          T.O. will also arrange for one Limber for
   Officers mess boxes and 2 limbers for trench kit,
   Cooks stores etc. to be at Bn H.Q. at 6 p.m.   Officers
   mess boxes and trench kits will be at Bn Dump at that time.
   1 servant per coy will remain in charge.

6. COMPLETION OF RELIEF.   Completion of relief will be
   notified to Bn H.Q. by code word "JACK".

7. ADMINISTRATIVE ORDERS.   Further Administrative orders
   are issued separately.

   A C K N O W L E D G E.

                              ....Captain
                              Adjt. 12/13th Northd Fusrs.

ISSUED BY RUNNER
AT 7.15 p.m
   27.1.18

          Copy No. 1 Brigade   No. 7 B Coy
                   2 10 Yorks R.   8 C
                   3 C.O.   9 D.Coy
                   4 Ward Diary   10 T.O.
                   5 File   11 Q.M.
                   6 A Coy   12 R.S.M.

ADMINISTRATIVE ORDERS

1. Advance parties from the Transport Lines will report at H.Q. 10th Yorkshire R. HEUDICOURT at 2.30 p.m. tomorrow. Strength: 1 C.Q.M.S. and 4 O.Rs. per Coy. The remainder of the Details not in trenches (less transport and Q.M.Store personnel) will parade under Major E.A.SCOTT in time to reach RAILWAY CAMP at 3.30 p.m. Parties will carry tea rations in haversack.

2. Lieut. H.W.DICKINSON, 2/Lieut. J.RICHARDSON and 2/Lieut. G.M.EDMONDS, M.C. will remain at the Transport Lines 2/Lieut. EDMONDS will take charge of any details which may be at the Transport Lines from the time the Battn is relieved. Details arriving will join the Battn at HEUDICOURT. as soon as possible.

3. Accommodation at HEUDICOURT will be alloted as follows:
   A, B & C Coys will each have one large hut.
   D Coy will occupy shelters in MIDDLESEX CAMP and sleep in the TUNNEL.
   H.Q. Details will be housed in FLEMING CAMP.
1 NISSEN Hut per Coy will be alloted to Coy Officers.

4. The Q.M. will arrange for hot tea and any unconsumed ration to be issued to Coys when they arrive (probable time 7.30 p.m. - 8.30 p.m.) The Sergeant Cook will be with the Battn after relief.

5. C.D Coy will detail 1 Lewis Gun team for duty at the anti-aircraft Lewis gun post in MIDDLESEX CAMP. This team will leave trenches at 2 p.m. and occupy a shelter near the post.

6. The Tommies tubs will be sent to Bn H.Q. by 3 p.m. Police will take charge of the Bath-house in which there will be one compartment for Officers and 3 sprays for the men.
   Baths will be alloted as follows:
   Tuesday   8 - 12 noon   A Coy
             1 - 5 p.m.   B
   Wednes.   8 - 12 noon   C
             1 - 5 p.m.   D
   Bootmakers, Tailors and Barbers will be sent forward with the Advanced parties and report at H.Q. at 2.30 p.m.

7. There are trenches outside the men's huts for use in the event of the Camp being bombed.

Routine.
   Reveille will be at   6.30 p.m. daily
   Breakfast   7.15 a.m.
   C.O's Orderly Room   9.30 a.m.
   Dinners   12.45 p.m.
   Teas   4.0 p.m.
   Rum when issued   8.30 p.m.
   Lights out   9.0 p.m.

The first day out will be spent in cleaning all clothing and equipment, haircutting, inspection of and repairing of boots.
   After the first day, Coy Commanders will arrange programmes of work to include:
   Arm Drill   9 - 10 a.m.
   Platoon drill   10 - 11 a.m.
   Anti-gas drill   11 - 11.30 a.m.
   Re-organisation into 4 platoons per Coy will be carried out on the first day out of the trenches.

............Captain
Adjt. 12/13th Northd Fusrs.

27.1.18

PRELIMINARY ORDERS for move tomorrow

The Battalion is to be relieved by the 16th SHERWOOD FORESTERS who will probably arrive about 11 a.m

The Battalion will be entraining about 12 noon at the Railway siding W.15.a.5.6 to proceed to MOISLAINS.

Companies will ensure that all the Camp and Huts are left in clean condition and will parade by Coys outside the Huts which will be left vacant at 11 a.m

(An advance party of one N.C.O. per Coy (preferably the C.Q.M.Ss if able to Cycle)) will report to Major White at Battalion H.Q. at 9 a.m with Cycles to go forward to the new area.

BLANKETS. One per man will be carried strapped on the packs, the remaining Blanket will be collected in Bundles of ten, labeled and stacked by Coys near Battalion Orderly Room by 9.45a.m. One N.C.O. per Coy will remain in charge of the Blankets.

The A/R.S.M will arrange for a guide to meet two lorries which are reporting at the CROSS ROADS W.15.d.0.8 (HEUDECOURT) at 6 a.m tomorrow to guide the Lorries to pick up Stores.

20.1.18.
(sd) J. McKINNON. Captain.
Adjutant 12/13th Northumberland Fusiliers

To. OsC. A.B.C and D Coys
H.Q. Mess. A/R.S.M.

Appendix 1

12/13th NORTHUMBERLAND FUSILIERS
OPERATION ORDER No 51.

SECRET
Copy No. 4..

Ref Map
62c. 57c
1/20,000

6th Feb 1918

1. **RELIEF**   The Battalion will take over the Camp of the 1st EAST YORKSHIRE REGIMENT at GURLU WOOD (D.29.a) tomorrow 7th instant.

       The Battalion (less Working party of 75 men per Coy) will parade at 2.15 p.m on Company Parade Ground to proceed to new Camp.

H.Q.   Order of March as per Margin.
A   DRESS. Full Marching Order.
B   ROUTE. X Roads D.18.c.5.8-X Roads D 20.d.0.4-
Drums   TEMPLEUX la FOSSE- CAMP at D 29.a
C
D

2. **ADVANCED PARTY.**   An advanced party of One Officer and CQMSs and one Runner of each Coy will go forward to report to H.Q. of 1st East Yorkshire Regt by 10 a.m tomorrow to take over Camp and arrange accomodation.-
       2nd Lieut C.H.R. DOMAN will proceed with this party

3. **WORKING PARTY.**   A Working party of 75 men and 3 Officers (including Company Commander) from each Coy, in full Marching Order will leave Camp at 8.30 a.m to proceed independently to positions in the GREEN LINE for work there commencing 10 a.m

       Coys will march with interval of 200 yds.

A.   Order of March as per Margin.
B.
C.   4. **TRANSPORT.** Transport will move ~~xxxxxxxxxxx~~ independently
D.   to LONGAVESNES tomorrow. The Lewis Gun Limbers will accompany the Battalion.

5. **OFFICERS KITS etc.**   Officers Kits will be at Q.M. Stores by 9.30 a.m Officers Mess Boxes will be at Battn H.Q. by 2 p.m

6. **BLANKETS.**   Blankets will be rolled in bundles of 10, labelled and stacked by Coys outside Coy Huts by 8 a.m
    Officers Kits and Blankets of the draft will be stacked ready for collection at Entrance to their Camp at 8.a.m

7. **LORRIES.**   Two lorries will probably be reporting at Church MOISLAINS at 1 p.m. A/Q.M will arrange for guides to meet the lorries and guide them to both Camps.

8. **DINNERS.**   Men remaining in Camp will have Dinners at usual time. Cookers will go forward to new Camp to have dinners ready for men on Working party by 2 p.m

9. **BILLETS.**   The Transport lines and all Billets and surroundings will be left in a clean and sanitary condition. The A/R.Q.M Sergt will remain behind to hand over Camp.

10. **DISCIPLINE.**   The strictest March discipline will be observed on the March.

11. **ACKNOWLEDGE**

Issued by Orderly at 8.15 p.m

Copy No 1   62. Inf Bde   .... Captain
       2   C.O. No 3 W.D.   Adjutant 12/13th Northd Fusiliers
       3   File.   5 A Coy
No 8 "D" Coy   6 B Coy   7 C
       9   T.B.   10   A/Q.M
       11   A/R.S.M   12   O.i/c Draft
       13.   O. C. H.Q Coy

Army Form C. 2118.

WAR DIARY
or
INTELLIGENCE SUMMARY.
(Erase heading not required.)

4-a

Place	Date	Hour	Summary of Events and Information	Remarks and references to Appendices
DISLAINS	1st		The Battalion was accommodated in 'A' Camp and cleaning of all equipment was favoured with and Companies re-organised into four platoons	
	2nd		2 O.R. joined from 'E' Depot. 2/Lieut. G. NOBLE rejoining after sick leave being posted to the Indian Army	
	3rd		Company training	
	4th		1 O.R. joined from 'E' Depot.	
	5th		Company training	
	6th		Company training 145 O.R. joined from 21 North Two. 2nd Lieuts. E.C. JONES, H.F. DODD, C.O. RAMSEY, W.S. BELL, T.W.T. RICHARDSON, R.M. MUSTARD, H.R. JOHNSON joined from 21 North Two. 22 O.R. joined from 21 North Two.	
EMPLEUX- FOSSE.	4/4		The Battalion moved to D.29.a. (Map Sheet 62 c NE 1/20,000) (6 reference the I.E. YORK.R. working on the Green Line. Operation Order No 57 is attached as Appendix 1.	Appx: 1.
	8th		Work on the programme was carried out on the Quartere. One Recon: by Coy was sent off duty for training.	
	9th			
	10		Lieut. Colonel R. HOWKETT Royal Fusiliers assumed command of the	

WAR DIARY
or
INTELLIGENCE SUMMARY.

(Erase heading not required.)

Army Form C. 2118.

Place	Date	Hour	Summary of Events and Information	Remarks and references to Appendices
TEMPLEUX LA FOSSE.	10th		Battalion on being re-posted from 10: YORK. R. and Lt-Colonel F.S. CHANCE proceeded on leave. Work on the Green Line and one Platoon for Coy training	
	11th		do	
	12th		The draft of 94 O.R. recently transferred from 1st South Fd. was re-distributed and a draft of the same strength recently transferred from 34th Div. was re-posted to this Bn. Work from 14 North Ju. (T) work on the Green Line and one Platoon for Coy training.	
	13th		do	
	14th		do	Training division
	15th		do	
	16th		do	
	17th		From 9.30pm until midnight the F.A. bombed the vicinity of the camp in a supposed effort to bomb Corps H.Q. two O.R. of the Batt. were wounded	
	18th		The Battalion was relieved by the 4 Leinster R who took over the work on the Green Line. The Battalion marched to MOISLAINS on relief. O.O. No 5R and Administrative Orders annexed as Appendix R	Appx R

Army Form C. 2118.

WAR DIARY
or
INTELLIGENCE SUMMARY.
(Erase heading not required.)

Instructions regarding War Diaries and Intelligence Summaries are contained in F. S. Regs., Part II. and the Staff Manual respectively. Title pages will be prepared in manuscript.

Place	Date	Hour	Summary of Events and Information	Remarks and references to Appendices
MOISLAINS	19/4		The Battalion paraded at 8.30am for Company training and was inspected whilst at training by the Army Commander (4th Army) who expressed his satisfaction with the appearance of the men and the arrangements made for training	
	20/4		Two Officers and 100 OR left for duty at ROISEL. Lieut & Q.M. HUXLEY 10 YORK. R. reported his arrival for duty	
	21/4		Company training	
	22/4		do	2/Lt CALDER reported to duty from 34th Division
	23/4		do	
	24/4		Sunday	
	25/4		Revielle and training	
	26/4		" "	
	27/4		Training Limits of Battalion and Brigade Frontier Explained	
	28/4		The Battalion entrained at Rlm to proceed to VILLERS FAUCON to relieve the 6th CONNAUGHT RANGERS 49 Inf Bde said HQ at RONSSOY	
			O.O. No. 54 and Administrative Orders are attached as Appendix 3	Appx 3

O.C.   A.B.C.D & H.Q.   T.O. & Q.M.

  With reference Operation Orders No 54. Guides as follows 1.Officer and 4 per Company will meet Companies at Road Junction F.21.a.8.8.   Sheet 8.2.c. at 5.30.p.m. and not as previously stated.

  Reference Administrative Orders of today, the Battalion will take over the Transport Lines of the 8th Connaught Rangers and not as previously stated.

                ....Capt.
27.3.18.   Adjutant.12/13th Northbn Fusiliers

Appendix 2

12/13th NORTHUMBERLAND FUSILIERS   SECRET
    OPERATION ORDER   No 52   Copy No. 5

Ref Sheets   Feb. 17th 1918
62c N.E.
and 57c
1/40,000

1.   The Battalion will be relieved by 7th LEICESTER REGIMENT tomorrow and will pass the Starting Point at 11 a.m.

ORDER OF MARCH :-   STARTING POINT:-
    "H.Q."   Road Junction. D.28.a.45.15
    "A"   Coy
    "B"   "
    "C"   "
    "D"   "

       Transport will accompany the Battalion and will take over the Transport Lines now occupied by 8th LEICESTER REGIMENT.

2.   Camps will be left scrupulously clean and Company Commanders will report the state of their Company lines to the Commanding Officer at the Starting Point.
       The strictest march discipline will be observed, blank files will be avoided.

3.   "C" Company will occupy the Machine Gun Camp at MOISLAINES, the remainder of the Battalion will occupy the same Camp as before, distribution of billets has been made known to all concerned.

4.   Dinners will be cooked on the March and will be issued 15 minutes after the arrival of the Battalion in Camp.

ISSUED BY ORDERLY AT 6 p.m
    Copy No 1   62nd Inf Bde.
           2   File
           3   W.D.
           4   C.O.
           5   2nd in Command.
           6   "A" Coy
           7   "B" "
           8   "C" "
           9   "D" "
         10   H.Q.
         11   A/RSM.
         12   T.O.
         13   A/Q.M

J W Elliott
.... 2nd Lieut.
Actg Adjutant 12/13th Northumberland Fusiliers

12/13th NORTHUMBERLAND FUSILIERS
ADMINISTRATIVE INSTRUCTIONS to accompany
Operation Order No 54 dated 27.2.18

1. **TRANSPORT.** The Battalion Transport will move tomorrow 28th inst to VILLERS FAUCON and take over Machine Gun Lines.

2. **RATIONS.** Rations will be delivered at Transport lines by VILLERS FAUCON.
   Q.M. will arrange for an N.C.O. to be at the Transport Lines by 10 a.m on 28th inst to take over rations for the following day.
   Rations will be brought up at night commencing 28th February to following Dumps:-
   For two Front Coys and Support Company GUILLEMONT Road (DUNCAN POST).
   For Reserve Company to KEN LANE via BASSE BOULOGNE.

3. **WATER.** Water will be brought up by Carts as follows:-
   Front Line and Support Coys to DUNCAN POST
   three tanks (300 Gallons)
   For "C" Coy to KEN LANE.
   Water Carts refill at Ste EMILIE at the SUGAR FACTORY
   The two Water Carts will require to make three journeys.

4. **R.E. DUMPS.** A forward R.E. Dump is kept supplied by the Field Coy R.E. for the RIGHT BATTALION, in GUILLEMONT Road just behind DUNCAN POST.

5. **BOMBS.** Battalion Store is in KEN LANE F.17.6.3.9.

6. **RETURNS.** List of returns required from Coys while in the Line is attached.

7. **S.O.S. SIGNAL.** S.O.S. Signal is a rocket bursting into two red and two Green Lights.

8. **REGIMENTAL AID POST.** R.A.P. is at DUNCAN POST.

9. **RATION CARRYING PARTY.** Each front line Company will detail a Ration Carrying party of one N.C.O. and eight men
   These should live in the neighbourhood of Company Cookhouses.

10. **GUM BOOTS.** Careful check of all Gum Boots must be made. All scattered Gum Boots will be immediately collected and returned to Battalion H.Q.

11. **OFFICERS VALISES, BLANKETS.** Blankets will be rolled in Bundles of ten, labelled and stacked by Coys outside Coy huts ready for collection by 9.30 a.m tomorrow.
    Officers Valises will be at Q.M. Stores by 11.30 a.m tomorrow.

12. **LORRIES.** Three lorries are reporting at MOISLAINS CHURCH at 1 p.m tomorrow 28th inst. Q.M. will arrange for Guide for lorries to be at rendezvous at 12.45 p.m

13. **Whale oil. Socks.** All men proceeding to trenches will carry out feet rubbing with Whale oil and change socks tomorrow morning. Q.M. will arrange for supply of dry socks to come up each night commencing 1st March. Q.M. will also arrange for supply of Whale oil to be sent up each night commencing tomorrow 28th inst.

14. **MEALS.** While in the line time of meals will be as follows
    Breakfast 7 a.m   Dinner 12 noon   Tea 4.30 p.m
    Hot Meal 12 Midnight

(sd) J. McKINNON. Captain.

Appx 3

12/13th NORTHUMBERLAND FUSILIERS SECRET
OPERATION ORDER No 54 Copy No. 2.
27.2.18

Ref Maps 62c 1/40000
"   "   62c N.E.2 1/40000

1. RELIEF. The 62nd Infantry Brigade will relieve the 47th Infantry Brigade in the Right Sub-Sector of the Divisional Front on 28th February.
   The Battalion will relieve the 6th CONNAUGHT RANGERS on the evening of 28th February in the RIGHT SUB-SECTOR of the Brigade Front as follows:-
   "D" Coy 12/13th Northumberland Fusiliers relieve "D" Coy 6th Connaught Rangers . RIGHT FRONT COMPANY
   "B" Coy 12/13th Northumberland Fusiliers relieve "B" COY 6th Connaught Rangers. LEFT FRONT COMPANY.
   "A" Coy 12/13th NORTHUMBERLAND FUSILIERS relieve "C" Coy 6th Connaught Rangers. SUPPORT COMPANY.
   "C" Coy 12/13th Northumberland Fusiliers relieve "A" Coy 6th Connaught Rangers. RESERVE COMPANY.
   Order of relief;- "B" "D" "C" "A". "H.Q"
   The Battalion will move by rail to VILLERS FAUCON arriving there at 5 p.m. Place and time of entraining will be notified later.
   DRESS. Full Marching Order.

2. GUIDES. Guides will meet Coys at Road Junction (F.21.c28) on outskirts of RONSSOY at 5.30 p.m
   NOTE. Two Platoons of 12/13th Northumberland Fusiliers will relieve one Platoon of 6th Connaught Rangers.

   Movement East of VILLERS FAUCON will be by Platoon at 200 yards interval.

3. TRENCH STORES etc. Programmes of Work, Defence Schemes, Maps, Trench Stores etc will be taken over and lists forwarded to Battalion H.Q. by 10 a.m 1sr March.

4. COMPLETION OF RELIEF. Completion of Relief will be notified to Battalion H.Q. by Code word "JACK"

5. LEWIS GUNS. Lewis Guns will proceed with Transport and will be stacked ready for collection by Coys at point on the Ste EMILIE-RONSSOY Road to be selected by L.G.O. and T.O.

6. ADMINISTRATIVE INSTRUCTIONS. Administrative Instructions will be issued separately.

   ISSUED by Orderly at 6 p.m
   No 1 Copy 62nd Inf Bde.
   " 2 File   No 3 W.D.
   " 4 C.O.   " 5 2nd in C.
   " 6 "A"   " 7 "B"
   " 8 "C"   " 9 "D"
   " 10 T.O.   " 11 Q.M.
   " 12 A/CSM H.Q.
   " 13 A/RSM.

                    .... Captain & Adjutant
                    for O.C. 12/13th Northumberland Fusiliers

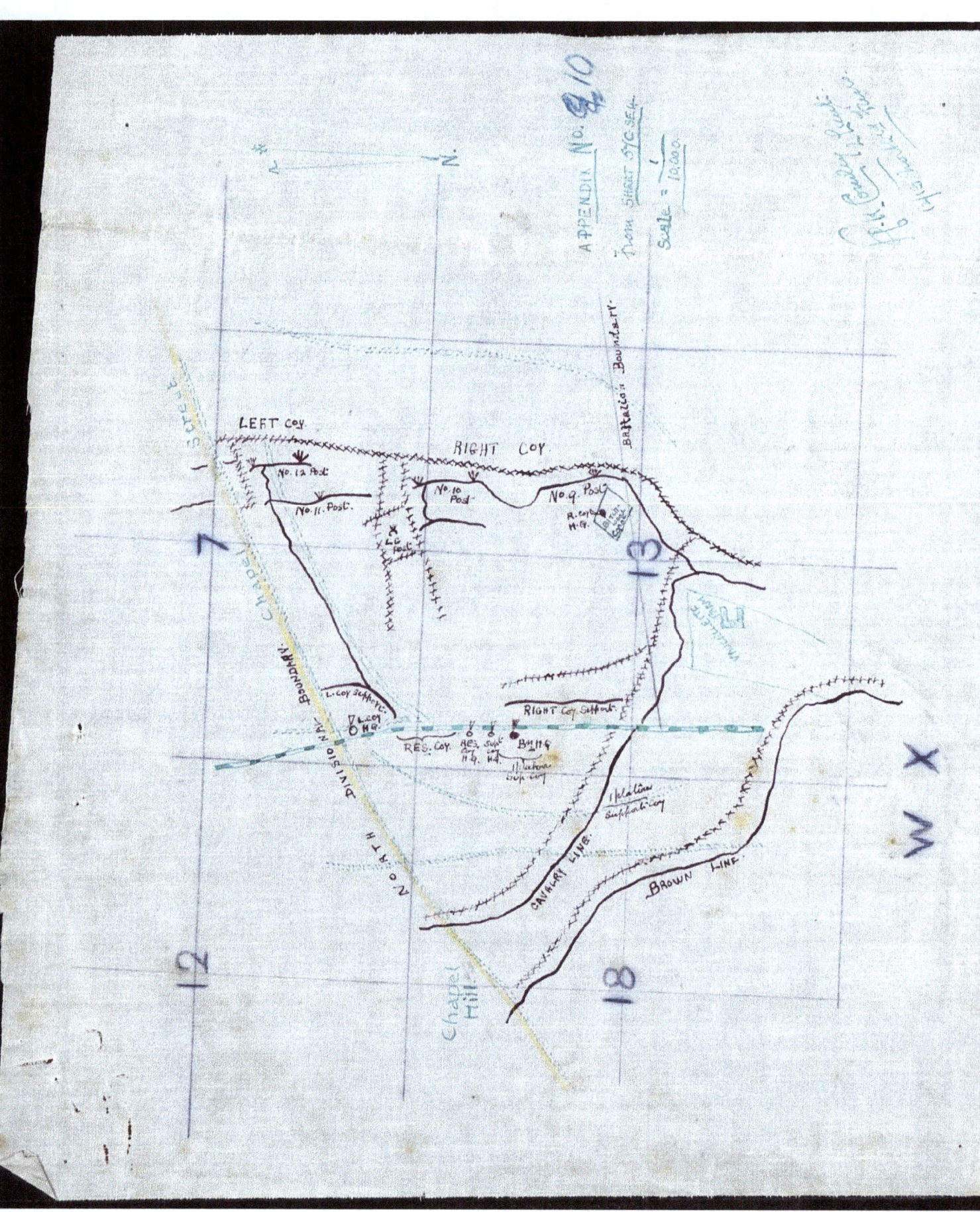

62nd Inf.Bde.
21st Div.

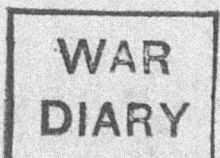

12th/13th BATTN. THE NORTHUMBERLAND FUSILIERS.

M A R C H

1 9 1 8

WAR DIARY
INTELLIGENCE SUMMARY.
(Erase heading not required.)

Army Form C. 2118.

12/13/NF 67/71

Place	Date 1918	Hour	Summary of Events and Information	Remarks and references to Appendices
TRENCHES NEUDECOURT	March 1st		Bn. occupied the left out-sector of the R.d.C. front. Capt. 2.R. Doe rejoined the Bn. from TRAINING CAMP, HAVRE	
	2nd 3rd 4th 5th 6th		The Battn. were relieved by the 2nd Lincolnshire Regt. and moved to NEUDECOURT (MIDDLESEX CAMP).	
	7th 8th 9th 10th 11th		General training was carried out during the time the Bn. was at rest. Lt. Col. R. Hewlett D.S.O. proceeded on leave on the 7th inst. and Major G. White M.C. assumed command. 21 O. Ranks joined from E. Depôt as reinforcements	8-9
	12th		The Battn. relieved the 1st Lincolnshire Regt. in the Right Out-picket of the Brigade front. 8 O. Ranks joined from E. Depôt as Reinforcements.	
	13th 14th 15th		Enemy remained very quiet and there was nothing of interest to report. At 11 p.m. (15th) a raiding party, about 100 strong, led by 2nd Lt. S. HUTCHINSON M.C. entered the enemy trenches. They succeeded in taking a number of prisoners and killed a good number of the enemy. Our casualties were 2 O.R. missing, 7 O.R. wounded.	
	16th 17th 18th 19th 20th		Nothing of interest occurred. The enemy was unusually quiet. After heavy bombardment the enemy attacked at 9.30 a.m. with very superior forces our right Coy. was overwhelmed	

Army Form C. 2118.

WAR DIARY
or
INTELLIGENCE SUMMARY.
(Erase heading not required.)

Instructions regarding War Diaries and Intelligence Summaries are contained in F.S. Regs., Part II. and the Staff Manual respectively. Title pages will be prepared in manuscript.

Place	Date	Hour	Summary of Events and Information	Remarks and references to Appendices
Green line to Bray	May 25		and they reach Battalion HQ. very quickly killing or taking prisoner the following officers Major J. White M.C., Capt E.H. Griffin D.S.O. M.C. Rev E. Loponcy, J. Wilkinson M.C. W. H. Elliott, 2/Lt Conley. B	
	Mar 25		The Bn fought rear-guard actions continuously from 6 a.m. until relieved on Mar 28. The following officers became casualties. Capt P.R. Shute, Capt Jo Byrne, Capt Deeming, Lt Amartal, Lt Hammond, 2/Lt Oonan, Richardson, Rupeno, Richardson R., Thompson, Copeland, Pringle, Mustard, Johnston D.L., Capt Violes ?, 2/Lt Williamson O.W.R. together with 424 O.R.	
Bray	Mar 26		A composite Bn under Lt Col R. Howlett D.S.O. M.C. was formed and at 5.30 p.m. left for Maricourt but was attached to the 35th Div. That night a withdrawal was made to the Bray - Albert line and the Bn dug in in front of Bray. Next day ...?	
	27 28 29		Next day a further withdrawal was made to the line of the Ancre where the Bn defended the village of Ribemont until relieved on Mar 29th.	
Bray - Ribemont	30 31		Bn was at rest in Heilly. Bn moved to Frechencourt & Pondainville.	

62nd Brigade.

21st Division.

12/13th BATTALION

NORTHUMBERLAND FUSILIERS

APRIL 1918.

WAR DIARY

INTELLIGENCE SUMMARY

Army Form C. 2118.

68/21

12/13th May 5th Inf.

9-a

Place	Date	Hour	Summary of Events and Information	Remarks and references to Appendices
HANGEST	April 1		Bn entrained for PESELHOEK and went from there by bus to LOCRE and Butler Camp.	
LOCRE	2		Reorganisation started. Draft of 173 O.R. joined from "East Yorks" Lt Ritzyma & Capt J.A. Riddell rejoined from England	
"	3		Reorganisation continued. Draft of 4 O. & 106 O.R. joined from England all A.H. Boys. Major Grad M.C. joined the Bn from England and took over 2nd in command. Capt T.B. M. Copestrant rector in command, 4th an Scott assume.	
WYTSCHAETE Reserve	4		Enemy very quiet. Some shelling of Camp Pat homes in evening.	
"	5			
"	6		Enemy Artillery slightly livelier. Capt OR Kingwood & 7 Lts Westerman & joined from leave.	
"	7		Bn was withdrawn to Butterfly Camp, LOCRE Area. Major A.S. Scott left for England.	
" CRIE	8,9		Training and reorganisation continued Bn moved to MOVIDA CAMP as reserve Bn to Reserve Bde. 258th	
"	10		They moved back to WYTSCHAETE and entrained in to Jul.	

Army Form C. 2118.

WAR DIARY
or
INTELLIGENCE SUMMARY.
(Erase heading not required.)

Instructions regarding War Diaries and Intelligence Summaries are contained in F. S. Regs., Part II. and the Staff Manual respectively. Title pages will be prepared in manuscript.

Place	Date	Hour	Summary of Events and Information	Remarks and references to Appendices
LINE WYTSCHAETE	11/12		Gap opposite the village after hard fighting this was accomplished. 80 O.R. became casualties.	
			Bn holding line. Very heavy shelling, enemy attacked in evening and was repulsed everywhere. Bn relieved by 9th Innis went to Report H Dug-Outs.	
Regent St Dug-outs Irish House	13 14 15		Left for IRISH House. 2 O.R. killed. Moved to line VIERSTRAAT – KEMMEL in afternoon. Went into line and relieved 2nd Innis.	
LINE WYTSCHAETE	16		After heavy bombardment enemy attacked and during to night turned our Right flank. A Defensive flank was then formed on high ground near Black Cot. following off. became casualties. Lt Col Howley DSO M.C. baptd. Lt. R. Seton-Browne, Lt Ritchie, Lt Dewsbar M.C. Relieved, Capt C.A. Lingwood, Lt Dolen, 2/Lt J. Gaitoon. 2/Lt Gotobed 2/Lt A.W. Dickman 2/Lt W.S. Bell, 2/Lt S. Lacey 11 G.R. & 320 O.R. D. Johnson 2/Lt G.P. Lacey, 9 320 O.R.	

WAR DIARY
or
INTELLIGENCE SUMMARY.
(Erase heading not required.)

Army Form C. 2118.

Place	Date	Hour	Summary of Events and Information	Remarks and references to Appendices
WYTSCHAETE	Oct 17		The remainder of the Bn held a defensive flank together with a Coy of 2nd Lincolns.	
do	18		The Bn in reserve in the same position and were withdrawn in the evening to SIEGE FARM.	
SIEGE FARM BOESINGHE	19		The Bn rested all day. B. Coy rejoined the Bn. Two officers and 5 O.R. wounded doing successful counter attack with the 2nd Lincolns on SPANBROEKMOLEN	
OUDERDOM	20		Bn moved to OTTAWA CAMP. Lt. Col. R.H. Alleman joined the Bn and took over command.	
	21		Reorganization of Bn started. R.S.M. Halloran 2.C.S.M. 20 others rejoined.	
	22		Reorganization & Lewis Gun training carried on. 2/Lts Williamson, Geggie & Stokes joined from 11th Northd Fus.	
	23		Reorganization carried on.	
	24		do. Heavy bombardment commenced at 2 p.m.	

Army Form C. 2118.

WAR DIARY
or
INTELLIGENCE SUMMARY.
(Erase heading not required.)

Instructions regarding War Diaries and Intelligence Summaries are contained in F.S. Regs., Part II. and the Staff Manual respectively. Title pages will be prepared in manuscript.

Place	Date	Hour	Summary of Events and Information	Remarks and references to Appendices
OUDERDOM	Sept 25		Very heavy gun fire commenced at 2 a.m. Stood-to at 4.45 a.m. and moved to Halifax camp. At 7 p.m. Bn was ordered to move up and relieve 1st Lincs in support. Bn moved up into Line Ridge Wood - Scottish Wood at 9 p.m.	
LINE RIDGE WOOD	26		Very heavy shell fire in afternoon. O.C. Bn. have asked 1st Batt. Stafft. batt. M.M. & Lewis total casualties 83 O.R. 3 Offrs. Godera wood evacuated. Bn relieved by 2 Mid Lines and kept platoon in vicinity of Ouderdom.	
	27		C.O. & two coys left for Busseboom in evening. Boy remained for D boy at 4 p.m. on line.	
OUDERDOM	28		Whole Bn to Busseboom. Severe casualties from shell fire.	
	29		Left by march route for STEENVOORDE camped in GERMOORDE WOOD.	
STEENVOORDE	30		Left by march route for KEDERZEELE Area. Major R.C. Wynter, M.C. joined Bn a/o & is in command.	

A.G. for O.C. 11/11/15 North Staffs

A.5834 Wt.W4973/M687 750,000 8/16 D.D. & L. Ltd. Forms/C.2118/13.

May 1918

WAR DIARY or INTELLIGENCE SUMMARY.
Army Form C. 2118.

1/13th K.L.R.

Vol 33

Place	Date	Hour	Summary of Events and Information	Remarks and references to Appendices
LEDERZEELE AREA	MAY 1		Battalion rested - Lieut C.R Wilson, 2/Lieut M.B Jackson and 2/Lieut W.J Musson joined the Battalion	
	2		Rest and bathing continued	
	3		Capt Murrough M.C. Lewis Black and makepeace joined from England - Major R.B Wynter took over second in command.	
	4		Battalion entrained at ARQUES at 6.45am - 2/Lieuts Heaney & Hund joined from 14th Northumbd and Lancers also Lewis Scott, Louthougle Pascoe Hanly Plantae Shuttleworth Robinson J.C. and Robinson W.S. Black and Collins from England.	
LHERY	5		Detrained at Boulouse and marched to Camp at LHERY	
	6		Battalion paraded at 9 am and did musketry and fire control - 2pm - 3 pm Physical training.	
	7 8 9 10 11 }		N.C.O.s drilled under R.S.M. Continued training	
LHERY to VAUX-VARENNES LINE	13		Battalion recieved 50 A.F. Chanceurs a pieds in COTE 108 Sector "A" Coy "y" in line "B" Support (close) - "R" & "B" Reserve Line very quiet. Serg.ts Bennington & Atkins awarded D.C.M. Lieut.Col R Hartell DSO awarded Bar to DSO	
	14			
	15		Line still quiet - 2 forwards "C" Company accidentally wounded.	

Army Form C.-2118.

WAR DIARY
or
INTELLIGENCE SUMMARY.
(Erase heading not required.)

Instructions regarding War Diaries and Intelligence Summaries are contained in F.S. Regs., Part II. and the Staff Manual respectively. Title pages will be prepared in manuscript.

Place	Date	Hour	Summary of Events and Information	Remarks and references to Appendices
BERRY-AU-BAC	May 16		Battalion still in line - very quiet. Inter-company relief carried out. B & A Coys relieved C & D Coys in front line and support	
	17		Battalion still in line. Inter coast relief and two support Coys and Headquarters bathed. Capt. Gleason joined Batt. from 4th/13th North'd Fusiliers	
	18			
	19			
	20		Inter Company relief. C & D Coys relieved B & A Coys in front line and support.	
	21			
	22		Line still very quiet. Reserve Coys bathed. Capt. Murray + Beuvardes and St Thomas to	
	23		report for duty.	
	24			
	25		Inter Company relief. B & A Coys to front line and support. C & D Coys to reserve.	
	26		Line still quiet. At 11 p.m. an alarm was given and all ranks to stand to in Battle Positions.	
	27		At 1 am the enemy put down a heavy barrage on our lines and put many gas shells. At 3:30 am enemy attacked and although the Barrows on left - The Battalion maintained their position on the main line of defence till ordered to withdraw to the CORMICY LINE. A further withdrawal to CHALONS WOOD was necessitated later in the day and at 8 pm the Battalion again withdrew to the ridge behind VAUX-VARENNES where the 62nd Brigade became Divisional Reserve. Casualties - Missing Capt. G.J. Gusson - Lieuts J. M'Coll F.B. Shakespeare, S.P. Brown. 2nd Lieuts D. Gregg, J.P.S. Fisher, Lt. Col. Brackman - P.S. golegan, Lt J. Bacon. B.S. Clarke, Capt. (R) J. Dunlop (R.A.M.C.). Wounded - 2nd Lieut P.W. Dunn.	
PÉVY	28		The Battalion took up a position on the MASSIF de ST THIERRY and maintained its position. Here in it withdrawal across the VESLE RIVER became necessary owing to the Enemy having worked round the right flank of the Division. In the evening the Battalion took up a position along a road EAST of JONCHERY with its left flank two yards west of SAPICOURT and its right flank in touch with the 2nd Lincoln Regt near VESLE RIVER	

WAR DIARY or INTELLIGENCE SUMMARY

Army Form C. 2118.

Place	Date	Hour	Summary of Events and Information	Remarks and references to Appendices
PENY	28		Casualties. Killed Capt. W.S. Broomhead. Missing 2nd Lieut. P.B. Davies. Wounded Lieut. G.B. Shanley.	
	29		The Battalion maintained its position during the entire day. In the evening about 8.30 p.m. the enemy attacked heavily and forced back the line. The Battalion stood and fought its way over the Somme. Casualties Killed - 2nd Lieut. W.F.L. Latham. Wounded - Lieut. B.B. Brown, 2nd Lieut. S.J.B. Stern & R.M. Bamborough. Battalion arrived at MARFAUX and joined the transport there. The Battalion moved by march route to VAUCINNES.	
	30		Total casualties from 29th to 29th - 18 Officers and 493 O.R.	
VAUCINNES	31		Battalion moved by march route to SOULIERS.	

(T. Slinn)
Lieut Colonel
Commanding 12/13th Northumberland Fusiliers

BEAR
OPERATION ORDER No 11.

SECRET
Copy No..2....
24.5.18

1. "A" Company will relieve "D" Company (H.Q. HENRIETTE)
   "B" Company will relieve "C" Company (H.Q. HENRIETTE)
   in the Line tomorrow night May 25th.
2. "B" Company will move off at 9.30 p.m
   "A" Company will move off at 10 p.m
   Platoons will be at 50 yards interval.
3. Guides and all particulars of relief will be arranged between O.C. Companies concerned.
4. All stores etc will be handed over on relief and lists sent to Battalion H.Q. as soon as possible.
5. Rations for "A" and "B" will be delivered at MOSCOU.
   "C" and "D" at Battalion H.Q.
   CQMSs for "C" and "D" will be at Battalion H.Q by 10 p.m to take over rations
6. Completion of relief will be wired by code word "EILLEN"
7. ACKNOWLEDGE.

ISSUED BY ORDERLY at 10 p.m.
Copy No 1. C.O.   Nos 2 & 3 W.D & File
No 4 A Coy No 5 B Coy   No 6 C Coy
No 8 R.S.M No 9 T.O.   No 10 Q.M.

.... Captn & Adjutant
BEAR

12/13 Northumberland Fusiliers

Operation Order No 5

Secret
Copy No 3
3rd May 1918

1. **TRAINS** The Battn will entrain at ARQUES tomorrow May 4th as follows:-
HQ. A. C. D and transport (less one Cooker) at 6.49 a.m.
"B" Coy and one Cooker at 2.49 p.m.
Personnel will report at entraining station 1½ hours, and transport 3 hours before trains are due to start.
Starting point and time of moving off will be notified later.

2. **Officers report to Entraining Officer** 2nd Lieut W P Ahern will report to entraining Officer ARQUES 3½ hours before departure of first train and Lieut Woodhouse 3½ hours before departure of second train with an accurate return showing number of Officers, other ranks, animals (by classes) and Vehicles (by types) which are to proceed by the train.

3. **Unloading party** "A" Coy will detail two Officers and 80 O.R. to act as unloading party at the detraining Station. This party will assist in unloading all trains, including Divisional Artillery.

4. **Billeting party** On arrival at detraining Station one N.C.O. per Company under 2nd Lieut W P Ahern will proceed on Bicycles to act as billeting party.

5. **Valises etc** All Officers kits must be on baggage wagons by 8 pm tonight. Officers Mess kit will be on Mess Cart by 9 pm.
"B" Coy Officers should put what will be needed for journey on their Cooker.

6. **Blankets** Blankets will be taken in the trucks with the men

7. **Billets and Camps**
   (a) All Camps, billets and horse lines must be left scrupulously clean. A Certificate to this effect will be obtained from the Area Commandant.
   (b) Tents and trench shelters will be left standing. A receipt for them will be obtained from the Area Commandant.
   (c) No tents or trench shelters except those allowed by Mobilization Store Table, will be removed from this Area.
   2nd Lieut M H Wilson will be in charge of above and will see that instructions are carried out.

8. Acknowledge.

Issued by Orderly at 4 pm
Copy No 1 62nd Inf Bde
" No 2 x 3 W.D. in file
" No 4 C.O.
" " 5 2nd in Command
" " 6 A Coy
" " 7 B "
" " 8 C "
" " 9 D "
" " 10 HQ "
" " 11 QM
" " 12 RSM
" " 13 2nd Lieut W P Ahern
" " 14 " " Woodhouse
" " 15 " " M H Wilson

Reinson Captain
Adjutant for O/C 12/13th Northumberland Fusiliers

12/13th Northumberland Fusiliers 11/5/18
Operation Order No 7

SECRET
Copy No. 2.

Reference 1/100000 Map
Soissons

1. The Battalion will march to the VAUX-VARENNES Area tomorrow.

2. (a) Order of March:- HQ "A" "B" "C" "D" Coys and Transport.

   (b) The Battalion will parade on Parade ground at 8.15am

   (c) All Baggage, including Officers kit and Blankets rolled in bundles of ten, will be stacked outside the Officers' Hut at 6.30am. Officers Mess kit to be outside the HQ Mess by 7am.

   (d) Orders as regards Billeting parties will be notified later

   (e) Dinners on arrival at VAUX-VARENNES - to be cooked on the march.

   (f) Water Bottles to be filled.

3. The strictest march discipline will be maintained

4. ACKNOWLEDGE

Issued by Orderly at 10.30 pm
Copy No. 1 62nd Inf Bde
        2 & 3 File & War Diary
        4   A Coy
        5   B "
        6   C "
        7   D "
        8   C.O.
        9   2M
        10 T.O.
        11 M.T.M.
        12 HQ Coy.

J. Pinson
Captain
Adjutant 12/13th Northumberland Fusiliers

12/13th Northumberland Fusiliers
Operation Order No 8

Secret
Copy No 2
13/5/18

1. The Battalion will relieve 50th Chasseurs a Pieds in the BERRY-au-BAC Sector tonight 13/14th May.

2. The Battalion will move off at 8.30 pm. Order of March. HQ "A" B "D" and "C" Coys. A distance of 50 yards will be maintained between platoons and no one will pass CHOPELLE before 9.30 pm. Dress Full Marching Order.

3. Guides as arranged between Company Commanders.

4. Rations and two Water Carts will leave at 10 pm
   "C" and "D" to MOSCOU
   "A" "B" Batt HQ & Water Carts to MARGUERITE

5. Lewis Gun limber will move off in rear of "B" Coy. Lewis Gun Officer will accompany limber and see that all Companies get their guns at Brigade HQ.

6. No smoking will be permitted after leaving Brigade HQ.

7. All water bottles will be filled.

8. All Officers Kit which they are leaving behind will be on transport by 6 pm.
   Officers Mess Kit will go up on ration wagons.

9. Completion of relief will be reported by runner at the earliest possible moment.

10. Acknowledge.

Issued by Orderly at 3.55 pm
Copy No 1 62nd Inf Bde
         2 & 3 File & W.D.
         4   C.O.
         5   A Coy
         6   B "
         7   C "
         8   D "
         9   HQ
         10   RSM
         11   QM
         12   TO

P. Hinson
Captain
Adjutant 12/13th Northumberland Fusiliers

SECRET

BEAR. OPERATION ORDER No 9...17.5.18

Copy No.........

1. A Coy will relieve D Coy (H.Q. COLETTE) and B Coy will relieve C Coy (H.Q. HENRIETTE) in the line tonight May 17th.
2. B Coy will move off at 9.30 p., using the overland track.
   A Coy will move off at 10 p,m using BOYAU ST MARTIN.
   Platoons will be at 50 yds interval.
3. Guides and all particulars of relief will be arranged between O.C. Coys concerned.
4. All stores etc will be handed over on relief.
5. CQMSs of C and D will come down ear;y and take over dug-outs now occupied by the Company which is relieving them.
6. Rations for A and B will be delivered at MOSCOU. C and D at Battalion H.Q.
7. Completion of relief will be reported by code word "BULLY"
8. ACKNOWLEDGE.

Issued by Orderly at 11 a.m
Copy No 1 C.O.
       2 & 3 File and W.D.
       4 A Coy
       5 B "
       6 C "
       7 D "
       8 R.S.M.
    9 Q.M.
   10 T.O.

.... Capt & Adjutant
BEAR

B E A R.   OPERATION ORDER NO 10.   SECRET.   Copy No 2
                                                           20.5.18.

1. "D" Coy will relieve "A" Coy (H.Q. COLETTE)
   "C" "   "   " "B" " (H.Q. HENRIETTE)
   in the Line tomorrow night 21st inst.

2. "C" Coy will move at 9.30 p.m, "D" Coy will move at 10 p.m.

3. Guides and all particulars of relief will be arranged between Company Officers concerned.

4. All stores etc will be handed over on relief and list sent to Battalion H.Q.

5. CQMSs of "A" and "B" will move down early and take over dug outs and rations which arrive at about 10.30 p.m.
   "A" and "B" at Battalion H.Q. "C" and "D" at MOSCOU

6. Completion of relief will be reported by code word "JEAN".

7. ACKNOWLEDGE.

Issued by Orderly at 6 p.m.
Copy No. 1. C.O. Copy Nos. 2 & 3 W.D. & File.
         4. A. Coy. 5 B. Coy. 6. C. Coy.
         7. D. Coy 8 T.O 9 Q.M 10 R.S.M.
                        (SIGNED) F. R. PEIRSON. Captn & Adjutant.
                                 B E A R.

Army Form C. 2118.

WAR DIARY or INTELLIGENCE SUMMARY.

(Erase heading not required.)

June 1918

12/13 th North Fusiliers

11-a

Place	Date	Hour	Summary of Events and Information	Remarks and references to Appendices
SOULIERES	1-6-18		The Battalion resting. A Company formed – consisting of 4 officers – Capt Murray, 2 Lt Blair, 2 Lt Robinson + Wilson – and 160 O.R's and proceeded to join the 21st Independent Brigade the next day – the 2nd	
"	2-6-18		Composite company paraded at 8 AM motor lorries at 8 A.M	
VILLEVENARD	3-6-18		A party consisting of 2nd Lt. Liddle Scaife + 5 O.R's proceeded to join the 21st I Bde as 1st reinforcements	
	4-6-18		The Battalion moved by Marvel route to VILLEVENARD and bivouacked outside the village.	
	4-6-18 5-6-18 6-6-18		The Battalion moved into the village. The men were spent in training – refitting. Capt Milson proceeded to take command of the 21st I.B. reinforcements at IGNY-LE-JARD	
	7-6-18 8-6-18		Training continued. Equipment was checked & cleaned with 2 Lt Godolphin + 160 O.R's proceeded to join the 21st I.B. as reinforcements. All the parties to 21st I.B. were moved by bus.	
LA NOCRE	9-6-18		The Battalion – with its transport – proceeded by marvel route to La Nocre starting at 10-20 A.M. and arriving in their billets there at 5:30 P.M.	
	10-6-18		The day was spent in cleaning up and getting men properly settled in billets.	
	11-6-18		All Officers received instruction in the Lewis gun. Lined instructors took the Lewis Gunners. Sig: paraded under the Signalling Officers	
	12-6-18 13-6-18 14-6-18		Lewis gunners + Signallers continued training. At 3 P.M the Battalion + transport moved by road to Etoanne Station arriving there at 5 P.M. Men were then served, and entrainment took place at 9 P.M. destination LONGPRES.	
LONGPRE	15-6-18		Arrived at Longpre station at 5 P.M. A meal was served here, then the Battalion + transport marched to HALLECOURT, billeted there for the night.	

WAR DIARY
or
INTELLIGENCE SUMMARY.

(Erase heading not required)

Army Form C. 2118.

Place	Date	Hour	Summary of Events and Information	Remarks and references to Appendices
HALLENCOURT	16-6-18		The day was spent at HALLENCOURT. Cleaning up.	
	17-6-18		The Battalion paraded at 11 A.M. and proceeded by march route to SENARPONT and billeted there.	
SENARPONT	18-6-18		Lewis gun training for Lewis gunners with and redistribution of billets took place. A draft of 4 J.O.R's arrived. 4 Officers (Capt Metcalf, Lt. g. Murthy, 2 Lt. E.J. Raynor & Lt. J. Stephenson) also joined. Later 14 O.R's joined from "O" cadre.	
	19-6-18		Reorganisation of Companies took place, whilst Signallers & Lewis gunners trained under their instructors. The Battalion was here.	
	20-6-18		The Independent Augusta Party reformed to-day and were here. 4 16 R's from 25 NF's joined, and 26 O.R's (Carsals) joined from "E" depot. The draft which joined yesterday were bathed. The Battalion paraded for drill, whilst Lewis Gunners & Signallers paraded under their instructors. 2 Lt. G. Mewett joined.	
GRANDCOURT	21-6-18		The Battalion paraded at 1-50 P.M. and proceeded by Gravel route to GRANDCOURT, which was reached at 8 P.M.	
	22-6-18		Companies paraded under O.C. Companies. Cleaning up & refitting was proceeded with. 2 Lts. R.L. Sully, R.G. Buringe & J.P. Foster joined the Battalion. Also 2 O.R's from "E" depot.	
	23-6-18		R.C's paraded at 9-15 A.M. & Rcd services in the Village Church. Arrangements were made for the opening of an Infantry & Lewis gun School for the Battalion to-morrow.	
	24-6-18		The Battalion School opened under 2 Lt. A & Seaife. 1 2 Lewis gun instructors, 24 O.R. O.s – 12 men being drafted under instruction. Battalion under Company arrangements.	
	25-6-18		Some Companies under their instructors in carrying out the Battalion under the new establishment. 3 O.R's joined from Base.	
	26-6-18	9 A.M – 12 noon.	The Battalion paraded as strong as possible for C.O. inspection after which Companies were at the disposal of Coy. Comms. Bathing by the Battn was practically carried out and the refitting of all ranks commenced. The Battalion was paid. 5 O.R's arrived from the Base.	

Army Form C. 2118.

WAR DIARY
or
INTELLIGENCE SUMMARY.

(Erase heading not required.)

Instructions regarding War Diaries and Intelligence Summaries are contained in F. S. Regs., Part II. and the Staff Manual respectively. Title pages will be prepared in manuscript.

Place	Date	Hour	Summary of Events and Information	Remarks and references to Appendices
GRANDCOURT.	27-6-18		The Battn. paraded at 9 A.M. for inspection by O.C. 62nd Bn. After inspection Companies carried on with musketry Coy- Platoon training under Coy arrangements. Lewis Gunners fired on the range. One Company fired during the afternoon.	
	28-6-18		Two Companies continued with Coy. drill while the other two, the Lewis Gunners fired on 30 yds range. Snipers continued training. Rifles inspected by Arm Sgt.	
	29-6-18		The Battn. paraded & marched to Villy-la-Bas for Divinal Service R.C. for C.of E. handed for respective services in ruins of R. Louts & Mitchell. R.Sields.	
	30-6-18		Joined Battn. Part of Transport moved to BEAUQUESNE by road.	

T Sharpin Lieut
O/C 12/13 Northfr

WAR DIARY
INTELLIGENCE SUMMARY

12/13th North [Fus?]
for the Month of July

Army Form C. 2118.

Place	Date	Hour	Summary of Events and Information	Remarks and references to Appendices
GRANDCOURT	1-7-18		Battalion Strength 35 Officers and 934 O.Rs. The Batt. paraded at 3 p.m. to march to LONGROY-GAMACHES remained by the new area. Weather hot.	O.R.
BEAUQUESNE	2-7-18			A.Rs.
"	3-7-18		The Batt. entrained at 4 am. and arrived at BEAUQUESNE at 6pm. Weather hot. Company commanders, one officer per company, and the Intelligence Officer reconnoitred around route to trenches in the vicinity of LAEVILLERS. The Battalion cleaned up. Weather hot.	O.R.
"	4-7-18		The B.O., Company commanders, Signal, Lewis Gun & Intelligence Officers moved off at 8 am. to reconnoitre the routes [approaches] to MAILLY-MAILLET returning at 12.40 in the afternoon. "A","B","C" Companies were inspected by the Adjutant in the absence of the C.O. In the afternoon "D" "HDQRS" Company were inspected by the C.O. At 10.30 pm a practice alarm was given & the companies were inspected at their respective alarm posts by the C.O. Weather again hot.	O.R.
"	5-7-18		All the Battalion fired two practices on 30 x range. During the intervals when not firing the P.T., B.F. under the Bn. P.T. Instructor [were held?] under Signal Officer. Weather hot.	O.R.
"	6-7-18		All the Battn. fired a Musketry practice on 100 x range. In the intervals company training was carried out. Weather fair.	O.R.
"	7-7-18		Battalion Strength 4 "Off" 932 O.Rs. The various denominations had	

Army Form C. 2118.

WAR DIARY
INTELLIGENCE SUMMARY.
(Erase heading not required.)

Instructions regarding War Diaries and Intelligence Summaries are contained in F.S. Regs., Part II. and the Staff Manual respectively. Title pages will be prepared in manuscript.

Place	Date	Hour	Summary of Events and Information	Remarks and references to Appendices
BEAUQUESNE	7-7-16		Church parade, with the exception of the Lewis Gunners who fired on the 30 x range. The G.O.C. 2nd Div. addressed everyone in the Battalion who had joined since March 21st of this year. Lieut O'Kern & 2/Lt. Hurd reynica from Lapine. The Adjutant & Adjutant made a reconnaissance of forward positions in the region of MAILLY-MAILLET. Weather fine.	Ackt/A.S.1
"	8-7-16		The C.O. Company Commanders, Intelligence, Signal & Lewis Gun Officers reconnoitred forward positions. "A" & "B" Coys. fired on the 300 x range. Lewis Gunners & Signallers trained under their officers. G. Sherwood joined the Battn. on the 2nd inst. Capt. Jack, 2/Lt. Hutchinson & Glendon joined on the 4th inst. 20% joined from "C" Depot today. & J.W.M. Greenwell proceeded to "C" Depot to join 17th Lancs Fus. Fired 1st practice on the 150 x range. Headquarters & Transport were trained. Lewis Gunners & Signallers trained under their respective officers.	Ackt
"	9-7-16		The C.O. lectured all officers excepting "C" & "D" Coys. The G.O.C. 5th Corps inspected the Brigade today & distributed medals afterwards. The Battn. marked past him. Weather showery.	Ackt
"	10-7-16		The Battn. fired two practices on the 300 x range. All the Battn. were S.B.R. for 1 hour. Weather fine.	Ackt
"	11-7-16		The Battn. fired on 150 x range today. There is a very appreciable improvement by the shooting since we arrived in BEAUQUESNE. The C.O. inspected the Transport this afternoon in the formation laid down in	W.L.

"A" Form
MESSAGES AND SIGNALS.

Prefix...Code...m.	Words	Charge.	This message is on a/c of:	Recd. at...m
Office of Origin and Service Instructions	21			
	Sent		...................Service.	Date...
	At ......m.			From ......
	To			
	By	(Signature of "Franking Officer")	By......

TO — BVMA

| Sender's Number. | Day of Month. | In reply to Number. | AAA |
| W.M.225 | 2. | | |

Hewitt WAR DIARY
for period 1st August 1918
to 31st August 1918.

From: HQHI
Place:
Time:

Censor.

WAR DIARY
INTELLIGENCE SUMMARY.
(Erase heading not required.)

Army Form C. 2118.

Instructions regarding War Diaries and Intelligence Summaries are contained in F. S. Regs., Part II. and the Staff Manual respectively. Title pages will be prepared in manuscript.

Place	Date	Hour	Summary of Events and Information	Remarks and references to Appendices
BEAUQUESNE	12-7-18		"Defence scheme administrative orders." There was a lecture given to the Officers on "Pigeons". Informed very interesting, but somewhat lengthy, so the Lecturer (a Corpl. R.E.) was a self enthusiast, "Pigeon man" in civil life. Wore S.D. for 1 hour. Weather fine.	A.L.
"	13-7-18		The Battn. route-marched for 8 miles. In the morning the Lewis Gunners & Signallers trained. Instruction under their Officers. We still wear our S.D. for 1 hour per day. Weather fine. Battn. Strength. 43 offrs. & 932 ORs.	A.L.
TOUTENCOURT	14-7-18		The Battn moved by march-route to TOUTENCOURT today & is now quartered in a camp. Things were very wet on our arrival & it still continues to shower.	A.L.
"	15-7-18		A much finer day, the camp is drying out. The Battn fired on 30ft range today. The Signal platoon practised communicating with aircraft. Good liaison was maintained during the practice. Lectures on range LSB's were given for 1 hour. The CO., QM., & Intelligence Officer reconnoitred Bn. HQ. & trench system in square 04 & 5.	A.L.
"	16-7-18		A tactical problem was set to Junior Officers & NCOs. A very hot day. The Bn. fired miniature range. "C", "D", Companies practised artillery formation. "HQ", "A", "B" companies latter & had a change of either Lewis Gun & Signal Officers reconnoitred trench system in square 04 & 5. The Battn fired on 100' range.	A.L.
"	17-7-18		Company commanders did a tactical exercise in the afternoon. Whilst on range coys. were LSB's for 1 hour. Lt. Col. Hartung CMG, DSO, joined the Battn. last night, also Capt. Milburn, Capt. Brenton M.C. rejoined.	A.L.

WAR DIARY

INTELLIGENCE SUMMARY.

Army Form C. 2118.

Place	Date	Hour	Summary of Events and Information	Remarks and references to Appendices
ARQUEVES	18·7·18		The Battn. paraded at 6.30 p.m. to march to ARQUEVES which was reached at 8 p.m. This morning "A" & "B" Coys. fired on the 30 ft. range, special attention being paid to slackness. "C" & "D" Coys. practised artillery formation.	O/c
"	19·7·18		The C.O. inspected the Battn. this morning after which the companies moved off to private parade grounds & dia company training. The Signallers fired on the range all the morning. The Army Commander inspected the Bttn. about in the afternoon. Weather fine.	do
"	20·7·18		Companies fired on the range during the day; in the intervals they did company training & more Sgt/Co. Lewis Gunners & Signallers trained under their officers. B men per company are now training under the Intelligence Officer as scouts.	O/c
"	21·7·18		Baro. Sivingts 45·6 ft. 9·44 OHs. Companies fired on the range wearing their SBRs. & did Musketry, judging distances. Lewis Gunners fired a the range. Signallers & Scouts trained under their officers.	do
"	22·7·18		Companies trained a parade ground 10 tow east per company fired on range. Lewis Gunner Scouts & Intell. continues.	O/c
"	23·7·18		The Battn. carried out training all the morning. In the afternoon Betweed a the organisation of the Nucleus party was dealt with. At 8 p.m. the Battn. officers dined at the "Hotel du Commerce", having for their guests, the G.O.C. 62nd Bde., F. The Batt. Major; the A.D.M.S. 21st Division & Major Waters V.C. of the 1st LINCOLNSHIRE Regt.	O/c

WAR DIARY
or
INTELLIGENCE SUMMARY

Army Form C. 2118.

Place	Date	Hour	Summary of Events and Information	Remarks and references to Appendices
IN THE LINE	24-7-18		The Battn relieved the ANSON Battn of the 63rd Div in the line in the MAILLY LEFT SECTOR. They moved off to a this at 3.15 p.m. & halted for a meal at ACHEUX enroute. A showery day.	A.H.
"	25-7-18		Nothing much happened. Vague information was sent in by Battn. O.P. We received a representative of the V Corps during the afternoon. Today we have had showers & as the trenches are not perfect they go into a bad state in places. Last night we had patrols out but no enemy were seen. Repairs were done to trenches.	A.H.
"	26-7-18		Free showery day. The trenches gave better. We did quite a good amount of wiring. Last night but evening patrols saw nothing. The enemy does not seem as if he wants to dispute our presence in "No Mans Land". The Battn strength 45 off & 933 O.R. A little finer today. More wiring was done last night. "No Mans Land" is our. Repairs were done to trenches.	A.H.
"	27-7-18		The Battn was relieved by the 1st & 2nd LINCOLNS, the relief went (very success)- fully. Arrangements ran up to Bde 149. All the Battn passed through this & some cases gas shells fell within a few feet of the men. 2/Lt Thompson received a very severe wound from one of these when but between his legs. The relief was complete by 3 a.m. & on arrival up to mn 1 off 2/Lt Thompson. The Battn 2/Lt R. Tully had died as the results of a	A.H.
IN RESERVE	27-7-18		...	A.H.

Army Form C. 2118.

WAR DIARY
INTELLIGENCE SUMMARY.
(Erase heading not required.)

Instructions regarding War Diaries and Intelligence Summaries are contained in F. S. Regs., Part II. and the Staff Manual respectively. Title pages will be prepared in manuscript.

Place	Date	Hour	Summary of Events and Information	Remarks and references to Appendices
IN RESERVE	29-7-18		Nil [received orders playing football on the 29/7/18]	O.H.
ACHEUX	30-7-18		The enemy again shelled MAILLY and the purple line with Gas & HE shells. Several of our bomb-proof shelters received direct hits from gas shells. All companies moved to ACHEUX dugouts station stating at 9am. The CO and Adjutant moved to ACHEUX & formed Headquarters there. Guides went to the 1/4 Turners Battn NF to guide companies into the line in the event of an attack. 2nd Lieut. B.A. Wilson joined the battalion from Divisional Wing along with 24 O/Rs. Casualties up to 12 a.p.m. 8 off & 126 men.	O.H.
"	31-7-18		The Battn at ACHEUX were all bathed & reclothed. 3 companies of Pioneers moved up to the purple system & came under the orders of Major Wipplis. Casualties up to tonight 2 off and 180 O/R. Strength tonight 10 39 off & 907 O/R.	O.H.

E.J. Greensway Lt Col
Comdg 12/13 N.F.

WAR DIARY
INTELLIGENCE SUMMARY

Army Form C. 2118.

12/13 NF 6/21

Place	Date	Hour	Summary of Events and Information	Remarks and references to Appendices
PURPLE LINE	1/8/18		Strength of Battalion — 39 Officers & 909 O.R.	
	2/8/18		2/Lt B.A. Watson and 24 O.R. joined from Divisional Wing. A fine day. The usual amount of shelling took place, the most prominent feature of the day being the great activity of enemy aeroplanes in the day and bombing squadrons at night. Weather fair. Enemy occasionally shelled MAILLY-MAILLET with shells of different calibres including some gas shells.	A/s
	3/8/18		Weather fair. Occasional shelling of MAILLY-MAILLET took place. At 9.15pm the Battalion took up position in front of BEAUSSART & obtaining No.1 Post BEGNA. The men were shelter & the night was spent in the open. The Battn held trenches amid continued showers of rain.	A/s
BEAUSSART	4/8/18		Rained on & off all day Battalion emptied trenches and "cleaned up."	A/s
	5/8/18		Quiet wet day. No movement during day. what little training =could be done was proceeded with. 2/Lt B.H. Gundry & 2/Lt A. Rayfield joined the Battalion and 2/Lt J.B. Doyle and 182 O.R. joined from "E" Depot. 10 men rejoined from hospital.	A/s
	6/8/18		Proved to be a dry hot day, and training was proceeded with, 2 companies per Battalion undergoing 2 hr training.	A/s
	7/8/18		Hot weather experienced. Quiet trenches evening. Strength of Battalion 43 Officers & 881 O.R.	A/s
	8/8/18		Working on the PURPLE SYSTEM, headquarters being in the BREWERY, MAILLY-MAILLET. In the afternoon the Battalion took up	A/s

13-a

WAR DIARY
or
INTELLIGENCE SUMMARY.
(Erase heading not required.)

Army Form C. 2118.

Place	Date	Hour	Summary of Events and Information	Remarks and references to Appendices
PURPLE LINE	9/9/18		Weather fair. During an advance from MAILLY - MAILLET, the enemy had been very quiet, but on return was signalised by a heavy bombardment of shrapnel, H.E.s & gas. (mustard & phosgene) 2/Lt. J.H. Hamilton and 29 O.Rs gassed from Divisional Wing. A fine warm day. The Intelligence Officer reconnoitred the Bd and although the Battalion went into the Trenches, having one company in the front line from TITAN AVENUE TO OLD BEAUMONT ROAD, one in support, one in right support, & one company in reserve. Headquarters were in a dug-out in TITAN AVENUE in Q2.d. 35.75 (Sheet 57 SE)	Off
"	10/9/18		The enemy was very quiet and the relief took place without a hitch. Counter fire this day. The enemy had been very quiet during the night, except for machine guns regularly sweeping the parapets off BEAUMONT RESERVE and OCEAN TRENCH. Enemy aeroplanes were active towards dusk.	Off
" in the Line	11/9/18		Weather again of the best. Improvements were made in the Trench system. L. R.G.C. Walker struck off strength on proceeding to Division at Keswick camp as Adjutant.	Off
"	12/9/18		Fine Friday. Enemy artillery active against BEAUSSART & MAILLY MAILLET. 150 C Div. in from Divisional Wing	Off
"	13/9/18		Weather again hot. No movement was reported yesterday and there were indications that the enemy was preparing to withdraw. At 3pm 3 patrols left our lines and two of them advanced about 1100 yards, the third patrol went on and gained contact about 1100 East of BEAUMONT HAMEL. Our men were the first of the Division to occupy or line overlook actual BEAUMONT HAMEL. Orders were came through to occupy today. Our forward company was done by Empty became a casualty, relieved by the 9 KOYS. OWN YORKSHIRE LIGHT INFANTRY late.	Off

WAR DIARY / INTELLIGENCE SUMMARY

Army Form C. 2118.

Instructions regarding War Diaries and Intelligence Summaries are contained in F.S. Regs., Part II, and the Staff Manual respectively. Title pages will be prepared in manuscript.

(Erase heading not required.)

Place	Date	Hour	Summary of Events and Information	Remarks and references to Appendices
In the Line	15/8/18		Battalion Strength. 43 Officers and 899 OR.	
"	16/8/18		Another fine day. Enemy artillery shelling in the vicinity of MAILLY-MAILLET. 13 OR. joined from Rein. Reinforcement Camp. Weather continued fine and hot. At night. Batln. Headquarters moved to MAILLY MAILLET, the disposition of the companies being as follows. "C" Company in OCEAN TRENCH from TITANS BUFFS. "A", "B", "D" Companies in Purple System from Q.P.C. 80.20 to Q.P.a. 89.10. Brigade Headquarters were relieved with 60 shells. A strong westerly wind sprang up and unmasked towards evening "D" company were relieved rather heavily. 3 direct hits on the trench being obtained. Enemy had no forward movements owing to the large area of trench occupied.	AW
Purple System	17/8/18		Weather cloudy, but remained fine throughout the day, rain falling at night.	AW
"	18/8/18		Weather same as yesterday. Rain at night.	AW
"	19/8/18		Another day during which the weather was unchanged. The Batln. moved to MAILLY kept ready to report for the attack. 2/Lt. L. Lydekker was transferred to	AW
"	20/8/18		Brigade Headquarters. I stood off at 8.30. p.m. (instant) Turned on the morning the Battalion moved to A. D'Ardigny.	AW
In the Line	24/8/18		In support to the 1st LINCOLNSHIRE REGT. Strength. 20 Officers 623 O.R. "A" "D" Companies in Support unit at 1 LINCOLNSHIRE REST. to take the BLUE LINE. "A" "D" Companies in Support moved to D'Ardigny. on the left and gained objective with 8 prisoners. Lewis was kept till D'Ardigny. on the right. The 142 Inf. Div. T by "A" comp. on the night until the 2nd LINCOLNSHIRE REGT., who had captured BEAUCOURT. At 10 p.m. "D" company went forward and formed last captured BEAUCOURT. At 10 p.m. defensive flank for the 1st LINCOLNSHIRE REGT. A. D'Ardigny.	AW

WAR DIARY
INTELLIGENCE SUMMARY.

Army Form C. 2118.

Place	Date	Hour	Summary of Events and Information	Remarks and references to Appendices
In the line	2/9/18 continued		relieved 2 companies of the 2nd LINCOLNSHIRE REGT. and took over the defence of BEAUCOURT, the relieving company being "A". 22nd Aug. Meanwhile "B" company had moved forward from point of assembly & had taken up a position WHITE CITY to ravine empty, at 3am. At 4.50am. they moved forward to WAGON LANE thence up LUMINOUS TRENCH & afte BEAUCOURT had been taken formed the front line and advanced to the railway embankment at R.Y.2.3. (57 D/SE), where they were held up by hostile machine gun & rifle fire, suffering several casualties. Fighting patrols were pushed across the ANCRE immediately, coming under heavy machine-gun fire. At 3.30pm the company moved the ANCRE, taking up position 50 yds behind BLUE LINE & "C" Company via LUMINOUS AVENUE reached the railway in R.Y.c, & with "D" Coy sent out a saddle patrol towards the BLUE LINE. This patrol in attempting to cross the northern side of the ANCRE marches suffered severe casualties & withdrew to the Railway Embankment. In the afternoon the company again crossed the marshes and reached a trench 100 yards behind the BLUE LINE & in spite of pushing up LITTLE TRENCH established a post in the BLUE LINE. This position was then taken up & positions in the BLUE LINE & Road remained in effect. Platoons were established with "B" Company on the left, but nothing which was established with "B" Company on the left, but nothing could be done in the night. At night patrols discovered the enemy totally gone. BATTERY VALLEY. During the morning Headquarters had been established in LUMINOUS AVENUE. Casualties during above operations were 10 OR rounded, 12 OR being evacuated sick.	All

WAR DIARY or INTELLIGENCE SUMMARY

Army Form C. 2118.

Place	Date	Hour	Summary of Events and Information	Remarks and references to Appendices
In the Line	22/8/18		Battalion strength 41 Off. and 880 O.R. Fighting strength 20 Off. 3-93 OR. "A" company was relieved about 3 p.m. and formed posts between "B" coy. in the BLUE LINE (R11.d) & the YELLOW LINE (R3.c.0). The remainder of "B" coy. took up a position in the road in R3.a. losing 1 Off. killed & 1 wounded during the operation. "B" coy. held the same position as on the previous day. Small enemy raiding parties were repulsed during the evening. A strong fighting patrol of "C" Coy. reached up LITTLE TRENCH and attempted to shell the enemy out of BATTERY VALLEY, falling owing to the superior strength. Headquarters remained in LUMINOUS AVENUE during the day. 2/Lt. Rowan was killed + 2/Lt. Williamson + 2/Lt. R. Mills wounded. [signed]	
	23/8/18		A + D companies with headquarters remained in the same position. B coy. in conjunction with "C" coy. took its objective in R3.b. & R.4.a. Losing two men until the enemy withdrew to cover like in R2.d. but she passed through, when the enemy engaged the enemy, and at night the advance fighting patrols of "C" coy. withdrew to NORTH of LUMINOUS TRENCH. Officer casualties were Capt. Milburn + 2/Lt. B.T. Lawton wounded. The Battn. moved the ANCRE + occupied the BLUE LINE till 9 a.m.; where it moved to that ridge at GRANDCOURT 1 p.m. The Battn. moved to the 64th Div. on our right the	
	24/8/18		forward to sunken road in R.9.c. Strong resistance met the 64th Div. b.m. left. At 7 p.m. positions were taken up in road R.12.a c. MIRAMONT, 42nd Div. on our left. Relieved the night where the Battn. remained the night	
	25/8/18		The Battn. under cover of mist moved forward in artillery formation with B.C. companies in the front + D + A coys. in support forming a rearguard at Z ES SARS ridge (M15a) + troops arrived at 2½ hours; where our Rolls reinforced until further orders were issued	

WAR DIARY
INTELLIGENCE SUMMARY
(Erase heading not required.)

Army Form C. 2118.

Place	Date	Hour	Summary of Events and Information	Remarks and references to Appendices
In the line	25/8/18		The enemy and the advance continued. Our final objective YELLOW CUT (N17c & N18a) was reached at 12.30pm. "B" Company captured 1 officer & 40 men at the BUTTE de WARLENCOURT. YELLOW CUT was found to be overlooked by the 63rd Div 9 "B" Coy got up position in BLUE CUT in N18b, "B" Coy had 2 Platoons in YELLOW CUT and A & D Coys remained in support. Batln H.Q. at N12 c 65.00. Lieut Murphy was killed, & the following officers were wounded:— 2/Lt A.W. Sterry & 2/Lt G. Mount (on transport when up by mine), 2/Lt Rayner & 2/Lt W.R.E. Sutton. "A" Coy (Lt. R.S. Turner) 2/Lt. ..... Rept non attd on R.E. Huff 10 OR casualties, "B" 11 killed & 12 wounded, "C" had 7 OR casualties & "D" Coy 12 OR killed & wounded. "A" Coy remained in support to 9am. Then moved forward taking over section in YELLOW CUT on the left of 1st LINCOLNSHIRE REGIMENT. "B" Coy consolidated position on road & "C & D" Coys occupied BLUE CUT. Bn Headquarters were situated at M18A 15.80 (Sheet 57d S.W.)	Att
"	26/8/18		The disposition of the companies was unarranged, "A & C" Coys being in YELLOW CUT & "D & B" Coys in right support respectively. At 9pm "D" Coy & "A C" Coys sent out two patrols each at 5.30 am. behind a creeping barrage to find out if the enemy had evacuated, Though N17a & N13 at & worked by the enemy. When 50x from the objective the patrols were subjected to heavy machine gun fire & bombs. The sunken road found to be strongly held by the enemy. Patrols returned to our lines at 6.45 am. On the night of the 24/29	Att
"	27/8/18		returned part of the 63rd Div. in BLUE CUT.	Att
"	28/8/18		the enemy was very active with his machine guns in front of us until about 11 pm. When he suddenly became quiet.	Att

WAR DIARY or INTELLIGENCE SUMMARY

Army Form C. 2118.

Place	Date	Hour	Summary of Events and Information	Remarks and references to Appendices
La Brie	28/8/16		Two patrols of "C" Coy. had been out in front in the earlier part of the night. Sgt Miller with the enemy. When the machine guns had been silenced a little counter patrol went out from N.Y.S.O. to & discovered that the enemy had vacated his position. The patrol returned at 11.45am on the 29th Aug. On the night 28/29 Aug. the Battalion was relieved by the YORKSHIRE REGT. The total casualties from the 2nd to 29th August were:- 10 Officers and 210 Other Ranks. Strength of Battalion.	
Bde Reserve	29/8/16		33 Officers & 965 OR. The Battn. marched from the line and bivouacked in old French system at Méaulte (afterns) 2/Lt W.S. Hutchinson rejoined.	
"	30/8/16		The Battn. found bivouacs, cleaned up & rested for the day. 2/Lt C. Weightman joined from 2nd/nd Wing. Capt. Ransom was struck off Strength - to England duty.	
"	31/8/16		Battn. proceeded to reorganise and refit. During the morning they did physical exercises. In the afternoon Capt. Rochford 2/Lt C. Ritson & 2/Lt Bowes joined from Divl wing with 150 OR. and 1 OR. from 4 NORTH. FUS. Strength at close of month 35 Officers and 899 Other Ranks. Transh Strength 22. Officers and OR.	

Commanders T. F. Jackson. Lt Col. Commdy 12/13 Northd Fus.

WAR DIARY
INTELLIGENCE SUMMARY.
(Erase heading not required.)

Army Form C. 2118.

2/3th. North. Fus.
for SEPT. 1918.
Vol 3
14-2

Place	Date	Hour	Summary of Events and Information	Remarks and references to Appendices
BRIGADE RESERVE	1/9/18		**Strength of Battalion** 35 Officers and 899 O.R. Weather fine. In the morning training was proceeded with, and in the afternoon bathing.	
	2/9/18		At 3 a.m. the Bn. moved, taking up position at WARLENCOURT, relieving the 2nd LINCOLNSHIRE REGIMENT. The day was fine and spent in rest. The Bn. moved again at 4 p.m. & 10 p.m. found them in position at N26d & N32b (Sheet 57cSW). On arrival bivouacs were made. One or two chaps shells fell in the neighbourhood, the Bn. suffering no casualty.	
	3/9/18		Weather undecided. The Bn. rested the day. 34 O.R. joined the Bn.	
	4/9/18		Weather fair. The Bn. moved at 8.30 a.m. and arrived in position in outer road at O20 a4d (Sheet 57cSW) at 11 a.m.	
	5/9/18		Fine & sunny until the evening when a thunderstorm broke out, lasting about an hour. At 9.30 p.m. the Bn. moved into bivvies at U10d (57cSW).	
	6/9/18		A hot day. Early in the afternoon the Bn. moved into position east of the CANAL DU NORD. The enemy heavily shelled our position during the day, and Capt. Murray D.S.O. 2nd Lt. Hutchinson M.C. Lt. Robinson, were 10 O.R. were rendered casualties. 2nd Lt. C. Wilkinson was struck off strength, going to France Two	

WAR DIARY
INTELLIGENCE SUMMARY

Army Form C. 2118.

Place	Date	Hour	Summary of Events and Information	Remarks and references to Appendices
BRIGADE RESERVE	4/9/18		At 6.30 am the Bn vacated their positions for the road W/4a – V25 b+d. (Sheet 57 d SE) The day was fine throughout and the Bn rested. In the evening the Bn moved forward in the valley in V26 a,c+d. 2Lts. G.S Moffat & J. Connah joined.	
	8/9/18		Strength of Battalion 33 officers & 896 OR. At 4 am "A" & "B" companies moved to reinforce the 2nd Lincolnshire Regiment in the front line whilst "C" & "D" companies reinforced the 1 Lincolnshire regiment. They were all in training by 6 am. At night Bn Hdqrs moved into the Brickyard at W21c. (Sheet 57 d SE) (Capt. G Palm, Capt. A Rutherford, Lieut. G.S. Moffat, & Lieut Glenwood wounded). The day was fair throughout. At night Bn Hdqrs & C & D companies were relieved and early next morning [2Lt. G Binns wounded]	
	9/9/18		arrived at [sketch] at V26 d (57 d SE). Bn Hdqrs & the two companies were relieved and rested. "A" & "B" companies were relieved at 9 am. Rain fell continuously throughout the day.	
	10/9/18		Weather again bad. The two remaining coys. A & B arrived at the tents at 1 am. They rested the night and were relieved during the day. Capt. AFS Lane, Capt. AG Mont. Lt Emmenson (Acy) until 37 OR.	
	12/9/18		Heavy rain fell throughout the day. We harnessed to Col. Shoeleraf DSO CMG Major Browther reported. 3/Lt. C.J Robinson struck off strength to 22 North two	
	13/9/18		Another wet day. P.T. & recreational training was proceeded with. 2/Lt R.W. Lindaugh reported with 94 OR	
	14/9/18		The day remained fine, in charge of a camp moved. The Bn was detailed. Training was proceeded with and two chaperones were inspected by Divl GAS OFFICER.	

WAR DIARY or INTELLIGENCE SUMMARY.

Army Form C. 2118.

(Erase heading not required.)

Place	Date	Hour	Summary of Events and Information	Remarks and references to Appendices
RESERVE.	15/9/16		Strength of Battalion 31 Offrs. 842 O.R. A fine sunny day. The Bn. paraded for training.	
In the line	16/9/16		Weather fair. At night the Bn. moved into the line, having one company in the front line in W.23.a., one in support in W.23.a., and two in reserve in valley in W.20.b & d., Bn. hdqrs. being in the Brickyard (Sheet 57ᵉ SE) 2ⁿᵈ Lieut's F. to R. joined.	
	17/9/16		Weather fair. At night enemy positions were taped out during afternoon to Roundagh during which period a heavy enemy barrage lasting half an hour was put down. Bn. hdqrs. left the Brickyard at 10 p.m. and arrived in new position in W.18.d.0.2 at 12 midnight.	
	18/9/16		By 2 a.m. the companies were in attacking positions. Between 2 a.m. & 5 a.m. the enemy patrols were laid out along the Bn. front, especially to the suspected strong points at cross roads in W.18.d.0.0 and W.22.b. to H.B. (57ᵉ SE), but all gathered no further information. At 5.24 a.m. the attack commenced, meeting a storm/curtain of rain. Both objectives were captured by 4.10 a.m., prisoners being 2 Officers & 183 O.R., and war material. Our casualties were 2ⁿᵈ Lt. Coyle & A.Lt. Connell wounded; 8 OR killed, wounded and missing. 2ⁿᵈ Lt. F.T. Rogers knocked off overnight. Lieut. S. Earnest took ???	
	19/9/16		During the night 18/19 A.B. & C. companys relieved the 1ˢᵗ LINCOLNSHIRE REGIMENT in the trench system named VAUCELETTE FARM. In the afternoon 'D' compy. moved to position in CAVALRY SUPPORT in W.18.d.a. At 11 p.m. the Bn. was relieved by 5ᵗʰ SCOTTISH RIFLES of the 33ʳᵈ DIVISION and marched to huts Lieut V.R. at C.(57ᵉ SE)	

WAR DIARY or INTELLIGENCE SUMMARY.

Army Form C. 2118.

(Erase heading not required.)

Instructions regarding War Diaries and Intelligence Summaries are contained in F.S. Regs., Part II. and the Staff Manual respectively. Title pages will be prepared in manuscript.

Place	Date	Hour	Summary of Events and Information	Remarks and references to Appendices
RESERVE	20/9/18		Showery & Windy. At 2pm. the Bn. paraded & marched to camp in U.4 (5Y C.Ls.) 2nd Lt. Offsomler & 20 O.R. joined.	
"	21/9/18		Weather again wet. The day was spent in reorganizing companies, cleaning up & improving tents. In the afternoon the Bn. was inspected.	
"	22/9/18		Fine day. Strength of Battalion. 30 Offrs. 824 O.R. 2/Lts. L. Morris, F.S. Inwood, R.W. Brand, H. Spenser joined the Bn. Weather wet. The Bn. paraded for baths & cleaned-up. 118 O.R. joined the Bn.	
"	23/9/18			
"	24/9/18		Fine weather prevailed. The Bn. paraded for an address by the BRIGADIER-GENERAL.	
"	25/9/18		A dismal day. The Bn. paraded at 1.15 p.m. & moved off via ETRICOURT, stopping for tea in the neighbourhood of Q5d. After this the Bn. moved into the line, relieving the 16th W. YORKSHIRE REGT. of the 92nd Brigade.	
In the line	26/9/18		The day was fine & fairly quiet. Zero was at 4.52 am. the Bn. gained its objective, but in the evening an enemy counter-attack. Capt. A.J. North, Capt. T.C. Coy, & 2/Lt. T.A. Mitchell were wounded & 7 O.Rs. killed & 35 wounded.	
"	27/9/18		At 9 am. the position was restored. The day proved wet. At 10.30 am. the patrols consisting of the Bn. Scouts and 1 platoon of 'D' Coy. left our lines. By 11 am. the patrol had reached GOUZEAUCOURT and by 11.15 am. had taken up a position commanding the railway, behind which the Germans were entrenched. The patrol returned at 1 pm. 26 O.R. joined the Bn.	
"	28/9/18			

Army Form C. 2118.

WAR DIARY
or
INTELLIGENCE SUMMARY.
(Erase heading not required.)

Instructions regarding War Diaries and Intelligence Summaries are contained in F. S. Regs., Part II. and the Staff Manual respectively. Title pages will be prepared in manuscript.

Place	Date	Hour	Summary of Events and Information	Remarks and references to Appendices
BOIS-ELEU-ARC	29/9/16		Weather fair. The Bn. moved to FAREM RAVINE and its environs, but later on in the day returned to AFRICAN TRENCH.	
	30/9/16		Weather fair. The Bn. moved up to Roll Sidings, taking up positions N.E. of GUNYEMER. Strength of Battalion was now 26 Officers & 808 OR. Total Casualties. Killed 43. Wounded 340. Missing 48.	

J. Brunton Lt. Colonel
Commanding 12/13 Bn; North'd Fus.

CONFIDENTIAL.

WAR DIARY

12/13th Bn Northumberland Fusiliers.

October 1st - 31st 1918.

Army Form C. 2118.

WAR DIARY
or
INTELLIGENCE SUMMARY. October 1918

(Erase heading not required.)

Instructions regarding War Diaries and Intelligence Summaries are contained in F.S. Regs., Part II. and the Staff Manual respectively. Title pages will be prepared in manuscript.

Place	Date	Hour	Summary of Events and Information	Remarks and references to Appendices
Brigade Res.	1/10/18		Battalion strength 21 Officers, 808 O.R. Battalion in Brigade Reserve.	
Nr GONNELIEU	2/10/18		Casualties for period from 27–30 Sept: 6 O.R. killed, 118 O.R. wounded, 118 O.R. missing. Battalion remained in Bde reserve.	
	3/10/18		Bde Sanit. Battalion relieved by 110th Bn. Battalion relieved by 1 Coy of Leicester Regt. & moved to bivouac west of GOUZEAUCOURT.	
GOUZEAUCOURT	4/10/18		The Battalion rested today.	
	5/10/18		The Battalion moved to position west of CANAL du NORD, near BANTEUX.	
L du N	6/10/18		Bde on demand march. 2/Lt Byam + 2/Lt Jackson from B. 1 advance party. 2/Lt Cornwell, Parnworth, Chatt, Smith, Licton + 150 OR joined Battn. The battalion moved off at 9.0 AM & took up position in the Hindenburg line, East of BANTOUZELLE. 3 OR wounded. Bn relieved by Division Reserve.	
	7/10/18		Moved to assembly position behind BEAUVOIR trench	

WAR DIARY
or
INTELLIGENCE SUMMARY.
(Erase heading not required.)

Army Form C. 2118.

Place	Date	Hour	Summary of Events and Information	Remarks and references to Appendices
In the Line	8/10/18		Weather fine. The battalion attacked WALINCOURT at 6 A.M. & gained objective at 6.0 p.m. Casualties. 2/Lt. V. Gibbon, 6/Phoris & 2/Trower killed. 2/Lt. 20 Townend, wounded. 2/Lt. O.R. killed 88 O.R. wounded. 22 O.R. missing. Major K.E. Wynter transferred to 15th France. Weather still fine. The 19th Bn. passed through at	
WALINCOURT	9/10/18	5.30 A.M.	carried on the attack. The Battalion billeted in WALINCOURT. Captain Woodridge M.C. 2/Lt. 9 Okipey & 6/Lt. Hughes 13 O.R. joined the battalion.	
	10/10/18		Battalion remained at WALINCOURT training & re-organising	
	11/10/18		Training & re-organising	
	12/10/18		Training & re-organising	
	13/10/18		Training & re-organising. Major K.E.D. Crescent M.C. & Lt. V. Bloomfield joined the battalion.	

WAR DIARY or INTELLIGENCE SUMMARY

Army Form C. 2118.

Place	Date	Hour	Summary of Events and Information	Remarks and references to Appendices
MAUROIS	14/10/18		Training & re-organising	
	15/10/18		Training & re-organising. 2/Lts W.A. Bradfield & J.F. Wilkinson & 34 O.R. joined the battalion. Strength 36 Officers & 668 O.R.	AB.
	16/10/18		Training & re-organising. 2/Lt O. Linnell & 107 O.R. joined	
	17/10/18		do.	
	18/10/18		The battalion training & re-organising	
	19/10/18		do.	
	20/10/18		Church parade	
	21/10/18		Including Reinforcements 39 Officers & 808 O.R. Strength. Battalion moved up to the INCHY	AB.
In the line	22/10/18		Battalion moved up to the INCHY. Parties reconnoitres, patrols &c.	
	23/10/18		Division attacked at 04.00 hours. The battalion moved from INCHY at 05.00 hours & went into divisional reserve west to AMERVAL. We followed up during the day as far as VENDEGIES. Casualties. Capt. Woodbridge wounded	AB.

WAR DIARY
or
INTELLIGENCE SUMMARY.

Army Form C. 2118.

Place	Date	Hour	Summary of Events and Information	Remarks and references to Appendices
In the line	23/10/18		The Brigade attacked at 04.00 hours. The Battalion passed through the 1st Bn the Lincolnshire Regt. at 06.00 hours & continued the attack. The 64th Bde on right being held up, "C" Coy our right flank Company could not get forward. Battalion attacked again at 16.00 hours & gained objective (X.11.a to X.11.D) Casualties 2/Lt R.A. Watson, O. Linnell, & J. Grunwell killed, 2/Lt H. Spence, J.T. Glatt, & A. Anderson wounded. 13 O.R. killed, 100 O.R. wounded, 30 O.R. missing.	JB
	23/10/18		Bde relieved by 110th Bde. The Bn moved to sunken road 3A – 2B	JB
	24/10/18		The Division relieved by 19th Division. Bn relieved by 10th B3 WEST YORKS & moved to rest at NEUVILLY at 14.00 hours.	JB
NEUVILLY	25/10/18		Battalion sent to baths. Incidents reported from WALINCOURT. ‡ J F [illegible]	JB
	28/10/18		Kit inspection & reorganising. Strength 38 Officers & 800 O.R. 2/Lts Horsley & Warkington, 2/Lts G.F. Carne & D. Gault + 124 O.R. joined the battalion.	JB

WAR DIARY
or
INTELLIGENCE SUMMARY.

Army Form C. 2118.

Place	Date	Hour	Summary of Events and Information	Remarks and references to Appendices
In the line	29/10/18		The battalion relieved the 10th Battn WEST YORKS at POIX DU NORD at 15.00 hours, & were reserve battalion of the Brigade. 2/Lt. Edwards joined the battalion.	
	30/10/18		Inspection of Rifles &c. 2/Lt. Gault + 9 O.R. wounded. 1 O.R. killed. The battalion still in reserve at POIX DU NORD.	
	31/10/18		2/Lt. Dyson + 3 O.R. wounded. Strength of battalion 35 Officers + 761 O.R. Total Casualties. Killed 50 Wounded 273 Missing 100.	903

J Brunton Lt Colonel.
Commanding 12/13 Northumberland Fusiliers

Army Form C. 2118.

WAR DIARY
or
INTELLIGENCE SUMMARY.   October 1918.
(Erase heading not required.)

Instructions regarding War Diaries and Intelligence Summaries are contained in F. S. Regs., Part II. and the Staff Manual respectively. Title pages will be prepared in manuscript.

Place	Date	Hour	Summary of Events and Information	Remarks and references to Appendices
Brigade HQ.	1/10/18		Battalion strength 30 officers 808 O.R. Battalion in Brigade reserve.	
NE GOUZEAUCOURT	2/10/18		Casualties for period from 27—30 Sept. 6 O.R. killed, 110 O.R. wounded, 1 O.R. missing.	JB
	3/10/18		Battalion remained in Bde reserve. Brigade Boundary relieved by 110th Bde. Battalion relieved by 1 Coy 4th Leicester Regt & moved to bivouac West of GOUZEAUCOURT	
GOUZEAUCOURT	4/10/18		The battalion rested today.	
	5/10/18		The battalion moved to position west of CANAL du NORD, near BANTEUX Bde in divnl reserve.	
La Lu…	6/10/18		At a short ½ hr. Notice, 15 agents S/adjutants & 15 Officers spoke in, The battalion moved off at 9 am + Capt. J. Mutch, Lieut Gibson + 15 Officers of Battn & took up position in support of Battn of Rifle Bde. the Hamburg Front East of BANTOUZELLE. Bde still in divnl reserve. 1 O.R. wounded	JB
	7/10/18		Moved to assembly position behind BEAUVOIR line in	JB

WAR DIARY or INTELLIGENCE SUMMARY

Army Form C. 2118.

Place	Date	Hour	Summary of Events and Information	Remarks and references to Appendices
In the line	8/10/18		Weather fine. The battalion attacked WALINCOURT at 6 AM & gained objective at 6.0 p.m. Casualties. 2Lt. J. Gibson, C.F. Morris & J. Fraser killed. 2Lt. J.O. Townend wounded. 2Lt O.R. killed. 28 O.R. wounded. 22 O.R. missing. 88 O.R. Wykes transferred to 15th R Fanes. Major F.C. Wykes transferred to 15th R Fancs.	JB
WALINCOURT	9/10/18		Weather still fine. The 17th Div. passed through at 5-30 A.M. & carried on the attack. The Battalion billeted in WALINCOURT. Captain Woolbridge M.C. 2/Lt G. Skipsey & 6 O.R. Rejoined 1/2/1 O.R. joined the battalion.	
	10/10/18.		Battalion remained at WALINCOURT training & re-organising	JB
	11/10/18.		Training & re-organising.	
	12/10/18.		Training & re-organising.	
	13/10/18.		Training & re-organising. Major F.E.D. Cressall M.C. & Lt. V. Bloomfield joined the battalion.	JB

WAR DIARY
INTELLIGENCE SUMMARY.
(Erase heading not required.)

Army Form C. 2118.

Place	Date	Hour	Summary of Events and Information	Remarks and references to Appendices
VALINCOURT	14/10/18		Training & re-organizing	
	15/10/18		Training & re-organizing. 2/Lt W. Bradfield & J. P. Williamson & 2/Lt O.R. joined the Battalion. Strength 36 Officers & 668 O.R.	JB
	16/10/18		Training & re-organizing	
	17/10/18		do. 2/Lt O'Donnell & 107 O.R. joined	
	18/10/18		The Battalion	
	19/10/18		Training & re-organizing	
	20/10/18		do.	
	21/10/18		Church Parade. Inspection Ammunition & 608 O.R. of B. Forms, Respirators, Feet &c Strength 39 Officers & 608 O.R. Battalion moved off to INCHY	JB
In the field	22/10/18		Given orders to attack at 04.00 hours. The Battalion moved from INCHY at 05.00 hours & went into Divisional Reserve and to AMERVAL. We followed up during the day in rear as VENDEGIES. Casualties Capt Woodbridge wounded	JB

WAR DIARY or INTELLIGENCE SUMMARY

Army Form C. 2118.

Place	Date	Hour	Summary of Events and Information	Remarks and references to Appendices
In the field	24/10/16		The Brigade attacked at 06.00 hours. The Battalion passed through the 12th Bn. at 06.00 hours eastward. The attack on right being held up by our right flank being enfiladed, could not get forward. Battalion attacked again at 16.00 hours & gained objective. (X11.a & X17.D) Casualties 2/Lts. R.G. Tatem, O. Durell, & J. Greenish killed. 2/Lts. K. Garner, S. T. Elliott, & A. Anderson wounded. 13 O.R. killed, 100 O.R. wounded, 30 O.R. missing.	JB
	25/10/16		Bn. relieved by 110th Bde. The Bn moved to sunken road JA-75	JB
	26/10/16		The Battalion relieved by 17th Division. Bn. relieved by 105 Bde. WEST YORKS & marched to Hut at NEUVILLY.	JB
NEUVILLY	27/10/16		Battalion had to take hutments vacated from WALINCOURT.	JB
	28/10/16		5th Inspection & reorganising. Below 9th, 36 Officers & 500 OR. Lts. Hosby & Wilkinson, 2/Lt. G.L. Caira & 2/Lt. T. Geer & 124 OR joined the Battalion	JB

WAR DIARY
or
INTELLIGENCE SUMMARY.

Army Form C. 2118.

Place	Date	Hour	Summary of Events and Information	Remarks and references to Appendices
In the Line	29/10/18		The battalion relieved the 10th Bat'n WEST YORKS at POIX DU NORD at 18.00 hours, & took over a battalion of the brigade. 2/Lt. Edwards joined the battalion.	JB
	30/10/18		Inspection of Rifles &c. 2/Lt Gull + 9 O.R. wounded. 1 OR killed en route at POIX DU NORD.	JB
	31/10/18		The battalion still in reserve at POIX DU NORD. 2/Lt. Ryan + 3 O.R. wounded. Strength of battalion 35 Officers + 761 O.R.	

Total Casualties.
Killed 50
Wounded 253
Missing 100

J Bowstead
Lt Colonel
Commanding 12/13 Northumberland Fusiliers

CONFIDENTIAL.

WAR DIARY

OF

12/13th Bn Northumberland Fusiliers.

FROM 1st November 1918. TO 30th November 1918.

WAR DIARY or INTELLIGENCE SUMMARY

Army Form C. 2118.

November 1918.

Place	Date	Hour	Summary of Events and Information	Remarks and references to Appendices
Forenoux	1/11/18		Bn strength 35 Officers and 761 O.R. Weather fine. Bn in reserve at POIX DU NORD.	
	2/11/18		Left POIX DU NORD at 1700 hours and proceeded to OVILLERS. Weather still fine. Bn occupying	
	3/11/18		Weather fine.	
	4/11/18		Left OVILLERS at 1200 hours and proceeded to ROUTE DE ECAILLON. Sheet 51 S.W. S.16.d.	
In the line	5/11/18		Very wet day. Moved forward at 0500 hours & pushed Divisional and commenced the attack on MORMAL FOREST. No opposition met in the forest. First objectives occupied at 09.30 hours. Pushed forward and encountered machine gun fire from the spurs on sheet 51 S.W. Squares 14 and 21. This we overcame and at 21 hours we occupied the sunken road in Square 15 and pushed forward patrols towards the SAMBRE CANAL.	
	6/11/18		Another wet day. 110th Brigade passed through us and we remained in support. Casualties during this action:— Killed 1 O.R. Wounded 5 O.R. died of wounds 1 O.R. Missing 1 O.R.	

Army Form C. 2118.

WAR DIARY
or
INTELLIGENCE SUMMARY. November 1915.
(Erase heading not required.)

*Instructions regarding War Diaries and Intelligence Summaries are contained in F.S. Regs. Part II. and the Staff Manual respectively. Title pages will be prepared in manuscript.

Place	Date	Hour	Summary of Events and Information	Remarks and references to Appendices
AYMERIES Belgium part of France Sheet 51 U.16	7/11/15		Weather very uncertain. At 10.50 hours the Bn. moved to billets in AYMERIES.	
	8/11/15		Inspection and reorganising.	
	9/11/15		Very fine day. Continual reorganisation.	
	10/11/15		Weather continuing fine and dry. Church parade and saluting drill. Football (with 6 company) in the afternoon.	
	11/11/15		Major T. McLachlan D.S.O. M.C., Capt Yeoman M.C. and Lieut Brown with 156 O.R. joined the Bn. today. Training under Company Commanders. Remaining hostilities signed arrangements. Weather still excellent. At 11.00 hours Bn. moved to BACHANT.	
BACHANT Belgium part of France Sheet 51 U.18.	12/11/15			
	13/11/15		Training under Coy arrangements. Afternoon devoted to sport in preparation for Divisional competition.	
	14/11/15		Weather very fine. Bn. in Mass under C.O. in morning. Sport afternoon.	
	15/11/15		Bn. moved to billets — AYMERIES.	

WAR DIARY
or
INTELLIGENCE SUMMARY.   November 1918.

Army Form C. 2118.

Place	Date	Hour	Summary of Events and Information	Remarks and references to Appendices
AYMERIES	16/11/18		Weather very fine. Physical drill, guards and Ransacking of arms dealt under Company arrangements. Afternoon devoted to preparation for Divisional sports, Boxing, cross country run, and tug of war.	
	17.11.18		Sunday. Weather still very fine and frosty. Bn. Church parades in morning, and afternoon for sport &c.	
	18.11.18		Training as before. Bn. paraded - Mass at 10:30 hours. Route marching by Companies ordered owing to expected march when Division moves from this area. Capt. T.G. FARINA, Capt. H.L. STAFFORD, Lt. G.M. PHILIP D.S.O. M.C. joined the Bn. today and 35. O.R.	
	19.11.18		Weather still fine. Parades and training as before. Lt. Col. J. BRUNKER M.C. assumed the D.S.O. and Capt. C.M. KOCH (attached T.M.B.) the M.C.	
	20.11.18		Parading and drills as usual. Strict attention is now being paid to clean arms and general discipline. Bn. Brig C.T. commenced series of lectures on Reconnaissance ... Reconnaissance afternoons.	

Army Form C. 2118.

WAR DIARY
or
INTELLIGENCE SUMMARY.   November 1918.
(Erase heading not required.)

Instructions regarding War Diaries and Intelligence Summaries are contained in F. S. Regs., Part II. and the Staff Manual respectively. Title pages will be prepared in manuscript.

Place	Date	Hour	Summary of Events and Information	Remarks and references to Appendices
AYNERIES	21.11.18		Weather very fine today. Regnal the Bn after Company parades for an hour turned in Mass and after a little ceremonial drill took march by Companies. Afternoon sport as usual.	
	22.11.18		Weather still excellent. Had Bn scouts march in morning. Fun and extd Bn musketry arrangements for our town.	
	23.11.18		Parades – Mass and drill ceremonial drill from 1030–1200 hours. Platoon football competition now in progress.	
	24.11.18		Sunday. Bn Church Parades – morning. Capt. LLEWELLEN, Lt. BOWIE & Lt. L. MOULD and 2Lt. E.F.G. FRIPP joined the Battn. today.	
	25.11.18		Wet day today. Route marching impossible but drill carried out as usual.	
	26.11.18		Weather fair. From 0900 hours to 1000 hours PT and drill under Company arrangements. At 1030 hours Bn paraded – Mass in full marching order and scouts march carried out.	

WAR DIARY
or
INTELLIGENCE SUMMARY. November 1918.

Army Form C. 2118.

Place	Date	Hour	Summary of Events and Information	Remarks and references to Appendices
AYMERIES	26.11.18 (cont)		Capt. F.G. MOORE, Capt. J. MILBURN M.C., Lieut. J.M. WILLIAMSON M.C. and 2/L H. RAYBOULD joined the Bn. today with 60 other Ranks.	
	27.11.18		Weather dull and foggy. Bn. under Company arrangements until 1030 hours. Bn. paraded in Mass and had ceremonial drill. CCE mid-day. Football etc. in afternoon.	
	28.11.18		Company arrangements (PT & Coy drill) until 10.00 hrs. Mass Parade 10.30	
	29.11.18		Company arrangements PT Coy drill 10.00hrs. Mass Parade 10.30 hrs route march. 6 Minors left Battn for examination at Cambrai.	
	30.11.18		Sunday. Church Parade in morning	

J.W. Heard Major

Commanding 13th Northumberland Fusiliers

CONFIDENTIAL.

WAR DIARY

OF

12/13th Bn Northumberland Fusiliers.

FROM:- 1st December 1918. TO:- 31st December 1918.

Army Form C. 2118.

WAR DIARY
or
INTELLIGENCE SUMMARY.
(Erase heading not required.)

for the month of December 1918

Instructions regarding War Diaries and Intelligence Summaries are contained in F. S. Regs., Part II. and the Staff Manual respectively. Title pages will be prepared in manuscript.

Place	Date	Hour	Summary of Events and Information	Remarks and references to Appendices
AYMERIES	1/12/18		Battalion Strength 46 Offs and 934 O/Ranks	
			Sunday Church Parade. Weather cold but dry.	98
	2/12/18		Training under Coy arrangements 1 hr PT. 30 O/Ranks (coal miners) left unit	98
			for examination at CAMBRAI. 16 Nco's left for substitution 30 casuals rejd	
			from Hospital.	
	3/12/18		Battalion paraded and marched to Pont sur Sambre to see the King who passed	98
			through to-day.	
	4/12/18		Training 0900hrs - 0930hrs PT 0930 - 1000hrs Arm Drill Mass Parade 10:30 50 O/Ranks	98
			(coal miners) left unit for examination at CAMBRAI.	
	5/12/18		Training 0900hrs - 1000 under Coy arrangements. Football during afternoon.	
	6/12/18		Training under Coy arrangements 0900 hrs - 1000 hrs Battalion Route March.	
			156 O/Ranks (coal miners) left unit for examination at CAMBRAI.	
	7/12/18		Training under Coy arrangements 0900hrs - 1000hrs Mass Parade 10:30 hrs for	93
			short route march.	
	8/12/18		Sunday Church Parades. Lieut Carr. Semple rejoined from Hospital.	
			together with 2 O/Ranks.	
	9/12/18		Coys at disposal of Coy Commanders. Educational Classes group "A" commenced	93
			4 O/Ranks rejd from Div Reception Camp. Men were bathed to-day.	

Army Form C. 2118.

WAR DIARY
INTELLIGENCE SUMMARY for the month of December 1918.

(Erase heading not required.)

Instructions regarding War Diaries and Intelligence Summaries are contained in F.S. Regs., Part II and the Staff Manual respectively. Title pages will be prepared in manuscript.

Place	Date	Hour	Summary of Events and Information	Remarks and references to Appendices
AYMERIES	10/12/18		Training under Coy arrangements from 0900hrs-1000hrs. 10.30hrs short route march full marching order. Football during afternoon.	93
	11/12/18		Weather exceptionally bad to-day. All parades cancelled, boys at disposal of Coy commanders, boys inspected by Commanding Officer in billets.	93
	12/12/18		Weather again very wet. Parades cancelled. Boys drew fresh linen and carried on with LB training in billets. 1 in 6 ranks (coal miners) left unit for examination at CAMBRAI.	93
	13/12/18		Weather still inclement. Route march cancelled. Training in billet. Weather brightened during afternoon and a football match was played.	93
	14/12/18		Battalion paraded for Route March. Full marching order.	93
	15/12/18		Sunday. Church Parades. Football in afternoon.	
	16/12/18		Boys under Coy arrangements. 1 hr PT N.C.O's 9mm recommended for promotion inspected by Commanding Officer. Preparations for to-morrows move.	93
	17/12/18		Battalion paraded at 0815 hrs and left AYMERIES at 0825 hrs by march route to ENGLEFONTAINE. Weather very bad. The Battalion was billeted here for the night.	93
ENGLEFONTAINE	18/12/18		Battalion paraded at 0645 hrs and left ENGLEFONTAINE at 0900 hrs march route to INCHY, arriving 1200 hrs. Weather very wet & windy making the march a hard one. Battalion billeted in INCHY for the night.	93

Army Form C. 2118.

WAR DIARY
or
INTELLIGENCE SUMMARY.
for the month of December 1918

(Erase heading not required)

Instructions regarding War Diaries and Intelligence Summaries are contained in F. S. Regs., Part II. and the Staff Manual respectively. Title pages will be prepared in manuscript.

Place	Date	Hour	Summary of Events and Information	Remarks and references to Appendices
INCHY	19/12/18		Battalion paraded at 05.45 hrs, and embussed at 06.00 hrs leaving INCHY at 0400 hrs for FOURDRINOY. The Battalion detrussed at 0400 hrs 2 kilometres east of FOURDRINOY and finished the journey by march route arriving at destination at 01.30 hrs.	83
FOURDRINOY	20/12/18		Day spent in cleaning and straightening billets which prove to be very poor. 2nd Lieut R.W. Bennett & 20 O.Ranks joined unit. 1 O.Rank (coal miner) left unit for examination at CAMBRAI.	83
	21/12/18		Boy's under Coy arrangements to-day. 1 hr P.T. Kit inspection. Buses inspected by Divisional General. Y.E.C.M. held to-day at Bde H.Q. PAVILION. 8 O.Ranks rejd unit from hospital.	83
	22/12/18		Sunday. Voluntary Church Services. Companies paid during afternoon.	83
	23/12/18		Boys under Coy arrangements. 1 hr P.Y. Coy Works Officers appointed for a work on repairing billets.	83
	24/12/18		Boys under Coy arrangements. 1 hr P.Y. 2nd Lieut A.S. Gault rejoined from hospital. Rugby match during afternoon.	83
	25/12/18		Christmas day. Church Services. Weather fine. Concerts, Whist drives, Competitions etc, arranged by Companies.	83
	26/12/18		Boxing Day. Weather fair. No parades or training.	83

Army Form C. 2118.

WAR DIARY
or
INTELLIGENCE SUMMARY. for the month of December 1918

(Erase heading not required.)

Instructions regarding War Diaries and Intelligence Summaries are contained in F. S. Regs., Part II. and the Staff Manual respectively. Title pages will be prepared in manuscript.

Place	Date	Hour	Summary of Events and Information	Remarks and references to Appendices
TOURDINOY	27/12/18		Battalion route march 0900hrs - 1200hrs. Weather bad. "A" Coy moved into Nissen huts.	8
	28/12/18		Lewis gun training carried out by Companies, 0900 hrs - 1200hrs.	8
	29/12/18		Sunday. Voluntary Services. Battalion bathed to-day.	
	30/12/18		Battalion bolours received. Training according to Programme. 09.00 hrs 12.00 hrs.	8
	31/12/18		Companies salvaging Battalion Area.	
			Strength of Battalion. 41 Officers 423 O.Ranks.	

J. Brunton. Lieut. Col.
Commanding 12/13 Northumberland Fusiliers

CONFIDENTIAL

WAR DIARY

OF

12/13th Bn. Northumberland Fusiliers.

FROM:- 1st January 1919.   TO:- 31st January 1919.

Army Form C. 2118.

WAR DIARY for January 1919
or
INTELLIGENCE SUMMARY.
(Erase heading not required.)

Instructions regarding War Diaries and Intelligence Summaries are contained in F. S. Regs., Part II. and the Staff Manual respectively. Title pages will be prepared in manuscript.

Place	Date	Hour	Summary of Events and Information	Remarks and references to Appendices
FOUDRINOY			STRENGTH OF BATTALION 47 OFFICERS 423 O.R.	
	1/1/19		Service for R.C's at 0800 hours. Bn. paraded in Mass 1030 hours. Farewell by General Gale commanding Brigade.	
	2/1/19		Weather very wet and foggy. No working carried out. Group of 30 hours to 12.30 hours. Fatigue work in our area consists of collecting old tins and setting up Barbed wire. (G.H.Q. Reserve Lines).	
	3/1/19		Two Companies training. P.T. and Handling of arms, and two companies salvaging their areas. 2/Lt. B.G. ALDERSON to Corps Construction Camp for Draft.	B
	4/1/19		Still very wet. Companies conducting a C.O. one O.R. Consounship Regulations scanned. Men to write their name and rank on envelope, liable to censorship at Base. 9 O.R. reptd. from Hospital. Lt. E.F.G. TRIPP and 50 O.R. to Corps Construction Camp for demobilisation.	B
	5/1/19		Sunday. - Voluntary Church Services. 2 Waterloo Details - i.e. men showing soldiers whose service expires between April 1919 and April 1920, to Corps Co. Camp. Meeting of Coy. Commanders - the afternoon for purposes of forming of Cadre. 4 Officers and 46 O.R. necessary for winding up purposes.	B

WAR DIARY
or
INTELLIGENCE SUMMARY.

Army Form C. 2118.

for January 1919

Place	Date	Hour	Summary of Events and Information	Remarks and references to Appendices
FOUDRINOY	6/1/19		Companies salvaging during the morning. Football and other sport during afternoon.	
	7/1/19		Wet day. Bn paraded strong as possible for address from G.O.C. Division. Parade cancelled owing to weather. Companies doing Lewis gun instruction - Lieut "D" Company returned up journey from Carleton.	
	8/1/19		Bn paraded strong as possible and marched to BOVELLES and were congratulated on their work during the last phases of the War by the G.O.C. Division. 4 O.R. rejd from hospital. 9 O.R. rejd from hospital. Usual Company & Union Company Commanders for salvage work.	
	9/1/19		Confrances nothing up to end the afternoon.	
	10/1/19		Two companies salvaging. Curfew wire and also drill in the morning. Palliasses now being issued and conditions gradually improving as more material comes to hand for billeting. Hover Lieut. 1 O.R. from hospital	
	11/1/19		Salvage in the morning and sport in afternoon. Tug of War team throwing and also Coverd. Soccer teams etc for Divisional sports which are expected to materialise very shortly	

WAR DIARY for January 1919.
INTELLIGENCE SUMMARY.

Army Form C. 2118.

Place	Date	Hour	Summary of Events and Information	Remarks and references to Appendices
FOUDRINOY	11/1/19 (cont.)		6 O.R. to Corps Concentration Camp for Demob[n]. 4 O.R. rejd. from Hospital.	J.B.
	12/1/19		Weather rather improving after a longish spell of wet murky days. The drainage of touring lines must be devised and such discomfort is therefore experienced. Fuel is difficult to obtain but in spite of this the men are quite cheerful. Recreation huts are being built and entertainment committees formed. 37 O.R. to Corps Con. Camp and 4 O.R. rejd. from hospital.	J.B.
	13/1/19		Rolling up started and will be carried out by companies. The Lewis Bn. & the Division today carried out a practice in receiving the King's Colour which is to be presented tomorrow. 2 O.R. to Corps Concentration Camp for Demob[n]: and 1 O.R. demobilised whilst on leave.	J.B.
	14/1/19		A colour-party of 120 O.R. under Capt. TRENHAM M.C. and two subalterns with Lieut. J.A. Unwin as colour-bearer proceeded to the Aerodrome at BOVELLES. Colour-parties for the other service Bns:– the Division i.e. 14" B. North'd. Fus. 6" and 7" Leicestr. Regt. 15" Durham Light Infantry and the 9" K.O.Y.L.I. were also present. The ceremony commenced at 11.00 hours. The Bishop of Leicester presented the King's Colour to each Bn. and the ceremony closed with a march past, with unfurled Colours. 5 O.R. to Corps Con. Camp for Demob[n].	J.B. (signature) Convenor

Army Form C. 2118.

WAR DIARY for January 1919.
INTELLIGENCE SUMMARY.
(Erase heading not required.)

Instructions regarding War Diaries and Intelligence Summaries are contained in F.S. Regs., Part II. and the Staff Manual respectively. Title pages will be prepared in manuscript.

Place	Date	Hour	Summary of Events and Information	Remarks and references to Appendices
FOUDRINOY.	15.1.19		Salvage work and settling up were carried out by Companies in the morning. Sport in the afternoon. 6 O.R. to Corps Con. Camp and 4 evacuated sick.	
	16.1.19		The majority of the B⁺ are now Turfs and much more comfortably settled. What drives at night find a large number of keen competitors.	
	17.1.19		Route marching in diff- outs and salvage work carried out. 1 O.R. to 11th B⁺. Weather getting rather frosty. Work on went as usual. Still a large amount of defence lines were to be taken in. 20 O.R. rejd. from hospital. Capt. T.G. FARINA evacuated to hospital. The B⁺ were balked — Pequigny.	
	18.1.19		Very fine frosty day today. 2 days being allotted.	
	19.1.19		Sunday. Voluntary Church Parades in morning. Remainder of men were balked at Pequigny.	
	20.1.19		"A" Coy. inspected in full marching order by Commanding Officer. Remainder of the B⁺ on salvage and diff E E. Lt. A.L. MOULD, 2Lt R.S.M. BOWIE and 59 O.R. to Corps Con. Camp for demob. 2 O.R. demobilised who to / on leave.	
	21.1.19		Two Companies route-marched, drill order (5 miles) and two on salvage. The Covington turned out 4400 tons of place today and 4400 tons. Divisional competition took	

WAR DIARY for January 1919.
INTELLIGENCE SUMMARY.

Army Form C. 2118.

Place	Date	Hour	Summary of Events and Information	Remarks and references to Appendices
FOUQUEREUIL	21.1.19 (contd)		Pte. Long won the Heavy-weight championship of the Division, and Pte. Nichol was second — the feather-weights	
	22.1.19.		Very hard frost making Company scout-marches dangerous. Two Companies scout-marched while two continued the rooffing up of Barbed wire. 6.O.R. to Corps Convalescent Camp for Demob. 10.R. evacuated sick. 30.R. sick from hospital. Sergeant Emery and Corporal McArdle awarded the Meritorious Service Medal.	
	23.1.19.		Companies drilling and reloading. Capt. Stafford struck off strength awaiting demobilisation — to Command Depot whilst on leave.	
	24.1.19.		Two Companies made scout-march, and two rolling up wire. Brig. General McCulloch P.S.O. D.C.M. lectured A & D Companies on "History". B & C Companies scout-marched. Lt. Temple evacuated to Eng. Cmd.	
	25.1.19.		H. Reive G. 271. Russell H. 271. Broadfield W.H. and 54 O.R. to Corps. Conv. Camp for Demob. 30.R. demobilised whilst on leave.	
	26.1.19.		Sunday. Voluntary Church Parades in morning. Snow falling during earlier part of the day. 2.O.R. demobilised whilst on leave.	

Army Form C. 2118.

WAR DIARY for January 1919

INTELLIGENCE SUMMARY.

(Erase heading not required.)

Instructions regarding War Diaries and Intelligence Summaries are contained in F. S. Regs., Part II. and the Staff Manual respectively. Title pages will be prepared in manuscript.

Place	Date	Hour	Summary of Events and Information	Remarks and references to Appendices
FOURIER	27.1.19.		B & C Companies route marched 8 miles. A and D settling up with. Football — A and D played during the night. 2/Lt Coston and 52 O.R. to Corps Concentration Camp for demob. 2 O.R. evacuated sick.	
	28.1.19		Companies employed in clearing their new area allotted previously.	
	29.1.19.		Owing to recent decrease in strength the Commanding Officer ordered A + B Companies to amalgamate and be called No. 1 Coy. and C + D to be so. 2 Coy. Hermann M.C. No. 1 under Capt. McKerlan R.S.O. M.C. and No. 2 under Capt. Hermann M.C. This was carried out during the morning. All sports are being postponed owing to the grounds being frost bound. 10.R evacuated sick.	
	30.1.19		All Companies route marched in drill order in morning. Company football match played in the afternoon.	
	31.1.19.		No. 1 Company route-marched and No. 2 had an hour P.T. and their ordinary ct a creche by Lieut Bloomfield. 1 O.R. demobilised whilst on leave. The following awards were notified in the New Years Honours	

Army Form C. 2118.

WAR DIARY for January 1919.
or
INTELLIGENCE SUMMARY.
(Erase heading not required.)

Instructions regarding War Diaries and Intelligence Summaries are contained in F. S. Regs., Part II. and the Staff Manual respectively. Title pages will be prepared in manuscript.

Place	Date	Hour	Summary of Events and Information	Remarks and references to Appendices
FOUDRINOY	31.1.19.		(continued).	
			The Military Cross. Captain H. DARGIE.	
			Captain F.R. DORE. Captain W.J. LOCK.	
			Mentions.	
			Captain H. DARGIE.	
			The Distinguished Conduct Medal.	
			15381 Corporal LUKE W.	
			Strength of Battalion at date:—	
			34 Officers, 469 O.R.	
			J Brunton Lieut. Col.	
			Commanding 12/13th North'd Fus.	

CONFIDENTIAL

WAR DIARY

OF

12/13th Bn Northumberland Fusiliers.

FROM:- 1st February 1919.   TO:- 28th February 1919.

WAR DIARY or INTELLIGENCE SUMMARY

Army Form C. 2118.

12/13ᵗʰ North'd Fus.   February 1919.

Place	Date	Hour	Summary of Events and Information	Remarks and references to Appendices
FOURDRINOY			STRENGTH OF BATTALION — 34 OFFICERS 469 O.R.	
	1/2/19		The morning was devoted to sport. 2Lt. R.W. BENNETT and 54 O.R. proceeded to Corps Concentration Camp for demobilisation.	
	2/2/19		Sunday. Voluntary Church Parade. In afternoon officers v N.C.O's at Shinty. Result Officers 7 - N.C.O's 2. - 2 O.R. demobilised whilst on leave.	
	3/2/19		Coys. 8 miles route march. Lieut. V. HORSLEY and 7 O.R. proceeded to Corps Concentration Camp for demobilisation. Bath. officers mess formed.	
	4/2/19		"A" and "B" Coy's. 1 hour P.T. and lecture by Brig Gen McCULLOCK. D.S.O, D.C.M. (G.O.C. 62ⁿᵈ Inf. Bde) on "History". "C" and "D" Coy's P.T and Ceremonial Drill. Hospital Admissions - 2 O.R.	
	5/2/19		"A" and "B" Coy's P.T and Ceremonial Drill. "C" and "D" Coys. 8 miles route march. Hospital Admissions 3 O.R.	
	6/2/19		Snow fell heavily during night of 5ᵗʰ/6ᵗʰ. Coy's clearing traffic routes all day. 62ⁿᵈ Light Trench Mortar Battery joined Batt. and came under the command of O.C 12/13 North'd Fus. for discipline, rations and billets. Capt C.N.G KOCK M.C rejoined the Batt. for duty. Lieut V. BLOMFIELD proceeded on special leave to England (Auth. A.C. 8658(o)) Hospital admission 1 O.R. 2 O.R. to Corps Concentration Camp for demobilisation.	

Army Form C. 2118.

WAR DIARY
or
INTELLIGENCE SUMMARY.   February 1919

(Erase heading not required.)

Instructions regarding War Diaries and Intelligence Summaries are contained in F. S. Regs., Part II. and the Staff Manual respectively. Title pages will be prepared in manuscript.

Place	Date	Hour	Summary of Events and Information	Remarks and references to Appendices
FOURDRIN	7/2/19		All Coys. P.T. and Ceremonial Drill.	
	8/2/19		The morning was devoted to sport. Capt R. TRENAM. M.C. proceeded on leave to England.	
	9/2/19		Sunday - Parade Service - Church of England - at 1100 hrs. Voluntary Service - Nonconformists - at 1115 hrs.	
	10/2/19		All Coys 8 miles route march. - In afternoon Bath. Muster parade. Lieut J. WILLIAMSON and 2/Lieut W. FARNSWORTH and 23 O.R. proceeded to Corps Concentration Camp for demobilisation. Capt T. McLACHLAN, and Lieut G.PHILIP D.S.O. M.C. and 1 O.R. proceeded to MEAULTE for duty with D.A.D.G + E. 3rd Army.	
	11/2/19		The morning was devoted to sport. Strength decrease. 2/Lieut J.P. WILKINSON (Auth AG 2158/9178(0) A/-8/2/19) 3.O.R. evacuated sick. 1 OR demobilised from Y Corps. School.	
	12/2/19		Batln Route March. Route Ref. Sheet 62E 40000 OISSY - Road Junction 0.10 d. 7.0. - Cross roads O.6. b. 80.95 FOURDRINOY. Strength:- Increase 2 O.R. from 62nd T.M.B. Decrease 3. O.R. to hospital.	
	13/2/19		No 1 Coy 0900 hrs - 1000 hrs. - P.T. 1000 hrs - 1200 hrs. Ceremonial Drill. Lieut F.H WORTHINGTON assumed the duties of A/Adjutant of the batn. vice Capt W J MORROGH. M.C. with effect from 13/2/19	

Army Form C. 2118.

WAR DIARY
or
INTELLIGENCE SUMMARY. February 1919
(Erase heading not required.)

Place	Date	Hour	Summary of Events and Information	Remarks and references to Appendices
FOUDRINOY	13/2/19	contd	Capt. F.R. DORE and 9 O.R. proceeded to Corps Concentration Camp for demobilisation.	
	14/2/19		Brigade route march. 8 O.R. proceeded to Corps Concentration Camp for demobilisation.	
	15/2/19		Baths at SAISSEVAL. 8 O.R. proceeded to Corps Concentration Camp for demobilisation.	93
	16/2/19		Sunday. Parade Service - Church of England at 1100 hrs. Voluntary Service - Nonconformist at 1100 hrs.	8
	17/2/19		Major K.E.S. STEWART M.C. reported from leave. All Coys. P.T. and Ceremonial Drill. Strength Increase 1 O.R. from A.P.M. 21st Div. 1 O.R. from Div. Canteen.	
	18/2/19		The day was devoted to sport.	
	19/2/19		A draft of 4 officers and 200 O.R. proceeded to join the 36th Battn. North'd Fus. 59th Div. Army of Occupation. (Auth. 3rd Echelon C.F. 177 d/- 8/2/19/-. Capt. G. METCALFE M.C., Lt. a/Capt. C.N.G. KOCH M.C., Lt. A.L. SCAIFE M.C., Lt. E. STEPHENSON.	93

WAR DIARY
or
INTELLIGENCE SUMMARY. February 1919.

Army Form C. 2118.

Place	Date	Hour	Summary of Events and Information	Remarks and references to Appendices
FOURDRINOY	20/2/19		All remaining details moved into main camp FOURDRINOY. Strength decrease 1 O.R. to hospital, 1 O.R. to Corps Concentration Camp, demobilisation, 1 O.R. to A.P.M.	
	21/2/19		In afternoon Officers v NCO's soccer. Result Officers 1 - NCO's NIL. Strength 1 O.R. increase from 3rd Army School.	
	22/2/19		In afternoon Officers v N.CO's soccer. Result Officers 4 - NCO's NIL.	
	23/2/19		Sunday Voluntary Church Parades. 9 O.R. to Corps Concentration Camp. 5 for demobilisation, 4 for re-inlistment leave.	
	24/2/19		In afternoon Bath v 1st Line Regt. Soccer. Result. Bath NIL - 1st Line Regt NIL.	
	25/2/19		Strength increase 1 O.R. from hospital. Capt R. TRENAM M.C. rejoined from leave.	
	26/2/19		Strength increase 1 O.R. from hospital. Strength decrease - Lt A.W. LAMBERT demobilised whilst on leave.	
	27/2/19		11 O.R. to Corps Concentration Camp for demobilisation.	
	28/2/19		Total effective strength 23 Officers and 132 O.R.	

J.G.Bruntz. Lt Col.
Commdg. 12/13 North'd Fus.

12/13th Batn. North'd. Fus.

Army Form C. 2118.

WAR DIARY
or
INTELLIGENCE SUMMARY.

March 1919

Place	Date	Hour	Summary of Events and Information	Remarks and references to Appendices
FOUDRINOY	1/3/19		Effective Strength of Battn. — 23 Officers + 132 Other Ranks	
	1/3/19		1 Officer (2 Lieut G.J. CARRIE) and 1 O.R. proceeded to join the 36th Battn. North'd Fus Army of Occupation. (Auth. 3rd Echelon wire C.R. N° S/9084/60 C. d/- 22-2-19)	
FOUDRINOY	2/3/19		Sunday. Voluntary Church Services. 1 O.R. to hospital in England.	
FOUDRINOY	3/3/19		Moving of stores and transport to Div. Cadre Park at LONGPRE. 2 Lieut H.B. GOULT proceeded on leave to U.K.	
FOUDRINOY	4/3/19		Moving of stores and transport to Div. Cadre Park at LONGPRE. Lt. Col. J. BRUNTON. D.S.O, M.C. proceeded to U.K. on duty. (Authority wire SPORTOLBO. SCB. d/- 25/2/19	
FOUDRINOY	5/3/19		Moving of stores and transport to Div. Cadre Park at LONGPRE. 1 O.R. to the Command Paymaster WIMEREUX for duty.	
FOUDRINOY	6/3/19		Moving of stores and transport to Div. Cadre Park at LONGPRE. 1 officer and 15 O.R. to Corps Concentration Camp; 1 officer for conducting duty (2 Lieut T.D. SMITH) and 150 R for demobilisation. 1 O.R. to C.O.O CALAIS	

Army Form C. 2118.

WAR DIARY
INTELLIGENCE SUMMARY.

March 1919

(Erase heading not required.)

Place	Date	Hour	Summary of Events and Information	Remarks and references to Appendices
FOURDRINOY	7/3/19		Moving of stores and transport to Div. Cadre Park at LONGPRE.	
FOURDRINOY	8/3/19		4. O.R demobilised whilst on leave.	
FOURDRINOY	9/3/19		Moving of stores and transport to Div. Cadre Park at LONGPRE.	
FOURDRINOY	10/3/19		Voluntary Church Services. 2Lt W.L. HOLMES proceeded on leave to U.K.	
FOURDRINOY	11/3/19		Battn. V. 1st Line R. at soccer. Battn. 3 - 1st Line R.O.	
FOURDRINOY	12/3/19		1.O.R. to hospital. Moving of stores and transport to Div. Cadre Park at LONGPRE.	
FOURDRINOY	13/3/19		3. O.R. to Corps Concentration Camp for demobilisation.	
FOURDRINOY	14/3/19		In afternoon Officers v N.C.O. + men at soccer. Result: Officers 5 - N.C.O. NIL.	
FOURDRINOY	15/3/19		1.O.R. rejoined from hospital.	
FOURDRINOY	16/3/19		Sunday. Voluntary Church Services. 1 O.R. from hospital and 1.O.R. from Div. Band.	
FOURDRINOY	17/3/19		Battn v 2nd Line Regt. at soccer. Result 2nd Line Regt 1 - Battn NIL.	
FOURDRINOY	18/3/19		2/Lt. C.W. HUGHES proceeded on leave to U.K.	
FOURDRINOY	19/3/19			

12/13TH BATTALION.

Army Form C. 2118.

WAR DIARY

INTELLIGENCE SUMMARY. March 1919.

(Erase heading not required)

Instructions regarding War Diaries and Intelligence Summaries are contained in F. S. Regs., Part II. and the Staff Manual respectively. Title pages will be prepared in manuscript.

Place	Date	Hour	Summary of Events and Information	Remarks and references to Appendices
FOURDRINOY	20/3/19		1. O.R. to hospital	
FOURDRINOY	21/3/19		1. O.R. from hospital	
FOURDRINOY	22/3/19			
FOURDRINOY	23/3/19		Sunday Voluntary Church Services	
FOURDRINOY	24/3/19			
FOURDRINOY	25/3/19		3 O.R. to D.A.P.M. 21st DIV.	
FOURDRINOY	26/3/19			
FOURDRINOY	27/3/19		1 Officer (conducting) 2 Lt. J.T. MITCHELL and 20. O.R proceeded to join 59th DIV. Army of Occupation. (Auth. 62nd Inf. Bde wire J.E.96 d/- 24/3/19)	
FOURDRINOY	28/3/19		1. O.R. from hospital	
FOURDRINOY	29/3/19		Sunday Voluntary Church Services 2 Lt. W.L.H. HOLMES proceeded to join 5.3rd Bn. North'd Fus. Army of Occupation. (Auth. A.G.2/58/9320(a)) d/- 21/3/19	
FOURDRINOY	30/3/19			
FOURDRINOY	31/3/19		Effective strength of Bsaltn. 21 Officers - 85. O.R.	

Hurleyash Major
Comm'dg 7/13 North'd Fus.

12/13th BATTALION.
NORTHUMBERLAND

Army Form C. 2118.

12/13th Battn. North'd. Fus

WAR DIARY
or
INTELLIGENCE SUMMARY.

April 1919.

(Erase heading not required.)

Place	Date	Hour	Summary of Events and Information	Remarks and references to Appendices
FOURDRINOY	1/4/19		Effective Strength of Batn. 21 Officers - 85. O.R. 9 O.R. joined from 14th Batn. North'd. Fus (Auth. 21st Div. 1279/200 d/- 25/3/19.	
FOURDRINOY	2/4/19		2 Officers Capt. T. McLACHLAN. D.S.O, M.C. Lieut. G.M. PHILIP. D.S.O., M.C. (att. D.G.R & E. 3rd Army) posted to 52nd Batn. North'd. Fus (Auth. A.G. 2158/9320 (O) d/- 19/3/19). 3. O.R. demobilised whilst on leave.	
FOURDRINOY	3/4/19			
FOURDRINOY	4/4/19		4 Officers Capt. F.G. MOORE, Capt. J.T. LLEWELLYN, 2 Lieut. B.I. ALDERSON, 2 Lieut. J.T. MITCHELL, and 1. O.R. proceeded to Corps Concentration Camp for demobilisation, and 7 O.R. to Corps Concentration Camp discharged to re-enlistment. Lieut. G.M. EDMONDS, M.C. to D.D.G.R & E. 5th Army on probation.	
FOURDRINOY BOUCHON	5/4/19		Batn. moved from FOURDRINOY to BOUCHON. Route CAVILLON - SOUES - HANGEST - CONDE FOLIE - BOUCHON. Lieut F.A. URWIN proceeded on leave to PARIS.	

WAR DIARY
INTELLIGENCE SUMMARY.

Army Form C. 2118.

April 1919

Place	Date	Hour	Summary of Events and Information	Remarks and references to Appendices
BOUCHON	6/3/19		Sunday. Voluntary Church Service. 2.O.R. posted to 14th Battn. North'd Fus. (Auth. 21st Div 1279/200 d/-3/4/19.) 2.O.R rejoined from 21st Div. Train R.A.S.C.	
BOUCHON	7/3/19		In afternoon Battn v 1st Wilts Regt. at Soccer. Result Battn 5. 1st Wilts Regt. 4.	
BOUCHON	8/3/19			
BOUCHON	9/3/19		2 Officers. Capt T. McLACHLAN. D.S.O, M.C. Lieut. G. PHILIP. D.S.O, M.C. taken on strength, posting to 52nd Battn. North'd Fus. cancelled. (Auth. A.G's A.G./2158/9320/(O) d/- 27/3/19. Capt. R. TRENAM. M.C., 2 Lieut. H.B. COULT. proceeded to England to report to Regimental Depot. (Auth A.G. 8658/(O) d/- 30/3/19. 2 Lieut H. RAYBOULD proceeded to join for duty 65. P.D.W. Coy. (Auth. D.A.G. A.G. 980/5 (M) d/- 5/4/19.	
BOUCHON	10/3/19			
BOUCHON	11/3/19			
BOUCHON	12/3/19			
BOUCHON	13/3/19		Sunday. Voluntary Church Service 1 Officer. Capt. W.J. MORROGH. M.C. and 3. O.R proceeded to Corps Concentration Camp for demobilization	

Army Form C. 2118.

WAR DIARY
or
INTELLIGENCE SUMMARY.

April 1919

Place	Date	Hour	Summary of Events and Information	Remarks and references to Appendices
BOUCHON	14/4/19		In afternoon Batn. v. Leicester Regt at Soccer. Result. Batn. 3 - Leic Regt 0.	
BOUCHON	15/4/19			
BOUCHON	16/4/19		22 O.R's posted to 36th Batn. North'd Fus., 59th Division, Army of Occupation. (Auth. D.A.G. wire C.F. 755 d/- 12/4/19.)	
BOUCHON	17/4/19		1 O.R. rejoined from hospital.	
BOUCHON	18/4/19		2/Lt T.D. SMITH. rejoined from conducting duties in U.K.	
BOUCHON	19/4/19			
BOUCHON	20/4/19		Sunday Voluntary Church Service. 1 Officer 2/Lt. T.D. SMITH, and 1 O.R. proceeded to Corps Concentration Camp for demobilization.	
BOUCHON	21/4/19			
BOUCHON	22/4/19			
BOUCHON	23/4/19		1. O.R. proceeded to join 36th Batn. North'd Fus (Auth. D.A.G. wire C.F. 755 d/- 12/4/19.	
BOUCHON	24/4/19		1. O.R. proceeded to join 36th Batn North'd Fus (Auth. D.A.G. wire C.F. 755 d/- 12/4/19. 1 Officer 2 Lieut C.W. HUGHES. attached to 1st Batn. Line Regt. pending posting to	

Army Form C. 2118.

WAR DIARY
— or —
INTELLIGENCE SUMMARY.

(Erase heading not required.)

April 1919.

Place	Date	Hour	Summary of Events and Information	Remarks and references to Appendices
BOUCHON AND LONGPRE	24/4/19	(contd)	The effective strength of Battn. on this date is 11 officers and 49 O.R. The Cadre of the Battn. consisting of 5 officers Major K.E.S. STEWERT. M.C., Lieut. F.H. WORTHINGTON, Lieut. F.A. URWIN., Capt. & D.M.J. LOCK. and Lieut A. DICKINSON M.C., and 37 O.R. entrained at LONGPRE at 1530 hrs for HAVRE	
HAVRE.	25/4/19		The Cadre detrained at HAVRE at 0515 hrs. and proceeded to No.1 Reception Camp, and late in the day moved to No.1 Despatch Camp.	
HAVRE.	26/4/19		6 officers and 15 O.R. loading transport on S.S. NOPATIN. at 1730 hrs and 5 officers embarked on H.S.S. HUNSLYDE. The Cadre proceeding to destination CATTERICK. prior to Southampton.	

[signature] Major,
Commdg. 13th of 13th Northd. Fus.

www.ingramcontent.com/pod-product-compliance
Lightning Source LLC
Chambersburg PA
CBHW080854230426
43662CB00013B/2105